A to Z of Classroom Behaviour

A to Z of Classroom Behaviour

of

TRACEY LAWRENCE

CORWIN

A SAGE Publishing Company

A SAGE company
2455 Teller Road
Thousand Oaks, California 91320
(0800)233-9936
www.corwin.com

SAGE Publications Ltd
1 Oliver's Yard
55 City Road
London EC1Y 1SP

SAGE Publications India Pvt Ltd
B 1/I 1 Mohan Cooperative Industrial Area
Mathura Road
New Delhi 110 044

SAGE Publications Asia-Pacific Pte Ltd
3 Church Street
#10-04 Samsung Hub
Singapore 049483

© Tracey Lawrence, 2019

First published 2019

Editor: Jude Bowen
Assistant editor: Catriona McMullen
Production editor: Nicola Carrier
Copyeditor: Diana Chambers
Proofreader: Sharon Cawood
Marketing manager: Dilhara Attygalle
Cover design: Wendy Scott
Typeset by: C&M Digitals (P) Ltd, Chennai, India
Printed in the UK

Library of Congress Control Number: 2018961569

British Library Cataloguing in Publication data

A catalogue record for this book is available from the British Library

ISBN 978-1-5264-6426-2
ISBN 978-1-5264-6427-9 (pbk)

At SAGE we take sustainability seriously. Most of our products are printed in the UK using responsibly sourced papers and boards. When we print overseas we ensure sustainable papers are used as measured by the PREPS grading system. We undertake an annual audit to monitor our sustainability.

TABLE OF CONTENTS

ABOUT THE AUTHOR

Tracey Lawrence is the Acting Head Teacher at Danemill Primary School where she has gained the reputation of being 'inspirational' from many of the parents. She is passionate about the children and families at the school, and she always puts the needs and happiness of the children at the heart of what she does.

Tracey leads the Behaviour module for the Inspiring Leaders SCITT programme, inspiring new teachers to put the sensitive and effective management of behaviour at the core of their teaching.

Out of school, she volunteers with a group for adults with special educational needs, providing opportunities for them to develop their organisational, social and creative skills, as well as fundraising to keep the group running.

Tracey's all-round skills show that she is a true advocate for the needs of young people, regardless of their background or needs.

Kindly provided by Julie Hickinbottom, Deputy Head at Danemill Primary School

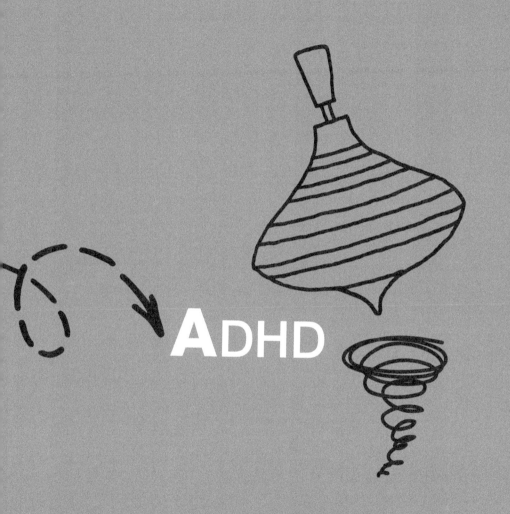

ADHD

When you talk to the majority of people, ADHD (Attention Deficit Hyperactivity Disorder) goes hand in hand with bad behaviour. It's the stereotype that many people spend lots of time trying to dispel. I can only assume that by buying this book, you have a mutual interest in finding out the reasons behind behaviour. By starting with exploring ADHD, I hope that it will enable you not only to feel empowered, but also to share these strengths with others.

The actual causes of ADHD are unknown, but current research suggests a complex interaction between environmental factors and genetic/risk predisposition. ADHD itself is a complex neurobiological condition that affects approximately 5 per cent of the population and significantly interferes with everyday life (Cooper, 2006). It is caused by an imbalance of some of the neurotransmitters in the brain. It is present from early on in childhood and is pervasive as it occurs in more than one setting – e.g., school and home. Diagnosis in childhood will usually be made after information from both settings and isn't usually made until after the age of 5. It often continues into adolescence and adulthood.

When ADHD comes up in discussion, it is often a controversial subject. Some even dismiss it as a condition that doesn't actually exist, but, regardless of people's thoughts and feelings, it is present in our schools, so we need to have practical ideas of supporting a child with ADHD as well as allowing them to reach their individual potential. The findings in research (Paloyelis et al., 2007) show that in people with ADHD there are differences within the development of the brain. The ability to control shifts from one activity to another, while the executive function and alertness differ from others. There is often a reduction in blood flow to the front of the brain. This area of the brain controls a variety of functions – e.g., emotions, memory, reactions to rewards and consequences, impulsivity and attention. Due to problems with neurotransmitters, messages are unable to complete their journey, causing children to present in a variety of ways – e.g., lacking in attention, argumentative, inappropriate behaviour, difficulty with schoolwork, difficulties with reading comprehension, poor memory, difficulties with retrieving information from memory, poor organisation. This list isn't definitive and research continues.

One of the most positive things you can do in your classroom is to be aware of the strengths that ADHD can exaggerate. In my experience, a child with ADHD can demonstrate the following positive strengths: charm, perseverance, resilience, tenacity, out-of-the box thinking, creativity, innovative thinking, a great sense of humour, musicality, being adventurous, intelligence, problem solving, risk taking, curiosity and a unique personality.

I would say that the most powerful strategy to implement in a classroom is to constantly support the difficulties a child with ADHD will face. This will be done by providing routines, repetition and boundaries. This will only be truly supportive of the child if all team members in your classroom are also consistent with this approach. Ideally, the whole school team will be able to provide this too.

To further support this, be explicit with the rules of the classroom and have them displayed in your classroom: words, pictures or both. Children with ADHD struggle to organise their time. You can support this depending on the setting. In primary, you can talk them through the structure of the day in the morning and reinforce this with a timetable. You can schedule points in the day for them to tidy up and organise themselves. At the end of the day, recap on the structure of the day so that they are clear. In secondary, you can buddy them up with somebody to talk through their timetable to ensure they are where they need to be during the school day. Check in with them in the morning to ensure that they have the right equipment. Deadlines will be a particular area of difficulty, so regular reminders and support in blocking out time will be vital.

The lack of structure that breaktimes and lunchtimes bring will be one of the main difficulties that you will face. Implementing routines, repetitions and boundaries will be the very basic support children will need. Some strategies that may provide support in a primary school include:

- having a key adult for children to speak to/to monitor their play;
- having a playtime diary to talk through their experiences;
- splitting lunchtimes by giving activities, such as attending computer club before free play;
- having a play buddy.

For the impulsivity, you need to be creative in providing opportunities for children throughout the school day to have a release. From my time in schools, physical exercise seems the most underused form of support and release. There are requirements in school such as sitting in our seats. We take for granted that children can do this, but for a child with ADHD, this can be harder than the learning. Allow children to have a break from the intensity of a long lesson by letting them give out resources, send a message to another teacher, run around the field – anything to satisfy that impulse and allow a child to remain calm for the remainder of the task. It can be the difference between a child struggling to even complete a task and creating a masterpiece.

CASE STUDY – Secondary – Imran – Year 9

Imran arrived at the school following an exclusion from his previous school. During the exclusion he received a diagnosis for ADHD. He was reintegrated into mainstream secondary school. As a school, they implemented the following strategies straight away:

- a communication method to help link home and school;
- regularly identifying any problem behaviour and becoming solution-focused in pursuit of supporting it (see photocopiable resource). Use the resource to identify the problem behaviour and the steps to support it as well as looking at rewards and consequences for this;
- a mentor to support organisational skills;
- responsibilities.

Imran was able, with these added supports, to thrive successfully in his secondary school.

In my experience, it can be common for children with ADHD to have a parent who has ADHD, so you may need to bear that in mind and think about ways in which you can help the family find wider support. It is important to note that there may be family members or siblings in the household without ADHD who would benefit from some work around emotions, but your individual school and situation will dictate how far you can help.

ATTACHMENT

Dr Maggie Atkinson, who was the previous children's commissioner (@matkinson956), believes that 'every teacher in every school' should be aware of attachment theory and tailor their practice accordingly.

It is important to make your classroom 'attachment-friendly' to ensure that you provide a safe and secure environment for all children to thrive. When you think of attachment, you think of John Bowlby, who conducted research into infant attachments in the 1940s (see www. simplypsychology.org/bowlby.html). Integrally, he found that although infants would go to anybody for food, they would only go to their mother when they were upset or frightened. If they could not get this, then it would create a trauma as they attempted to develop a range of strategies for survival. He found that the way the children view the world is based on the care they receive and this influences their later interactions. He termed this as the 'internal working model'. With a child who had an insecure attachment, they might feel bad, worthless, unwanted, incapable of being loved. They are more likely to feel that any caregivers are hurtful and untrustworthy, and that the world is dangerous. If a child has experienced insecure attachments in their life, where they have not been able to rely on an adult to respond to their needs, they may not have been able to learn how to manage their emotions, develop confidence and engage in positive relationships. This may present itself in challenging behaviours in the classroom.

In order to have an 'attachment-friendly' classroom, there are some strategies that can be implemented in both a primary and secondary setting:

- Positive language – a similar technique that you can use with a child displaying challenging behaviour. Ensure that all staff use positive language in your school – e.g., 'I can see that you are upset, Maria. Put down the chair so that we can talk about it.'
- Key adult/mentor – this is particularly appropriate at unstructured times to provide support for children during times that they may not feel emotionally ready for – e.g., friendship issues at lunchtimes. This provides options of support and advice for challenging situations.
- A familiarity around Theraplay principles – a small group intervention conducted by specialists. It can be perceived as controversial, as it involves putting children into situations that they may have missed in early life.
- Safe space – have a safe space in your primary classroom or a safe space in your secondary school for a child to go to where he or she can debrief after an unsettled period. Have the option for something to eat/drink. When a child is struggling and self-regulates, it often leaves them dehydrated.
- Constantly revisit with your members of staff to have an unconditional positive regard for children. It is imperative that children have a sense that they are liked and will be liked.

Must follow on Twitter:

@AUK_Schools – Attachment and Schools – UK

Primary – Case Study – Fred – Year 1 (aged 5)

Fred is a boy in Year 1 who was adopted at the age of 3. The reason for the adoption was due to neglect within his birth family. This had a variety of effects on Fred, some of which were unseen. His adoptive parents were seeing difficult behaviours displayed at home, with issues around control, and were seeking support from the school as well as the virtual head team.

Theraplay was introduced as an intervention for Fred in school, to try to provide those building blocks that may have been missed in early childhood. Theraplay was developed in the 1960s in America and is a form of focused therapy designed to enhance attachments between parents

4

and children; activities are playful, fun and developmentally enhancing and are designed to be practised with a therapist as well as at home. They include:

- lullabies;
- patty-cake (also known as pat-a-cake).

Must follow on Twitter:

@ADHDSolutionsUK – keep reading current research around ADHD and working with agencies like @ADHDSolutionsUK who will be able to support you on a case-by-case basis.

REFERENCES

Cooper, P. (2006) 'Assessing the social and educational value of AD/HD', in M. Hunter-Carsh, Y. Tiknaz, P. Coooper and R. Sage (eds) *The Handbook of Social, Emotional and Behavioural Difficulties*. London: Continuum, pp. 248–63.
Paloyelis, Y., Mehta, M., Kuntsi, J. and Asherson, P. (2007) Functional magnetic deficit hyperactivity disorder (ADHD): a systematic literature review. Available online at: www.ncbi.nlm.nih.gov/pmc/articles/PMC3763932

Problem Behaviour

Strategy	Strategy	Strategy

Rewards	Consequences

BEHAVIOUR

Behaviour – the very reason why you purchased this book. The difficulty we face in the classroom is that there are so many different forms of behaviour. Type 'behaviour' into social media and you will see a tornado of arguments. Within these there is a common theme: behaviour is getting worse. I honestly don't feel this is true. Behaviour is becoming more present in daily life because we are talking about it and it is no longer the elephant in the room that nobody dares to discuss. Don't get me wrong – I still believe that we leave it too late to talk it through, but there is no rapid decline.

Behaviour is different from person to person. Boundaries differ. Ways of dealing with behaviour, understanding behaviour and what each person tolerates are different. By unpicking the different behaviours, we can identify the difficulties more quickly and focus on solutions and support.

Low-level behaviour is one of the most common behaviours that we see in both primary and secondary mainstream schools. It is among the highest reasons that teachers cite for leaving the profession. We explore this further in the 'L' entry. We will look at case studies and strategies to minimise low-level disruption in the classroom.

Behaviour for Learning is ensuring that a child is ready for learning. Until a child feels safe and secure, and consistently able to behave within the boundaries of a school setting, they are not ready to learn the content that you are intending to teach.

CASE STUDY – Secondary – Mrs Banks – Year 8

Mrs Banks has a class of 28 Year 8 children. They are middle ability but are predicted to be higher ability. There is a small group of five children whose behaviour is preventing them from learning at the rate that they need to. Other children in the class are influenced by this behaviour and exhibit low-level behaviours.

Mrs Banks raised the subject of the problem behaviour with her colleagues and discussed it in her departmental meeting. Other teachers were having similar experiences. They discussed two options that they decided to move forward with. The first option was the use of positive behaviour management as a way of engaging children and modifying their attitudes. It had a direct impact on the children's behaviour and engagement in sessions, so much so that they began to discuss it further in school and the positive behaviour approach was used more widely.

The positive behaviour strategies implemented that had a direct input on this change in behaviour were:

- postcards sent home with positive messages;
- verbal 'direct' praise;
- merits for the correct choice of behaviour;
- stickers in planners towards a positive behaviour treat;
- visual reminders when children were getting off-task;
- rewards from the head of department/principal.

The second way forward discussed by the teachers was ensuring that motivators were planned into lessons. Motivators that they planned in the lessons included:

- a 'hook' into lessons to engage, inspire and motivate the children;
- a challenge for all;

- individual/group work;
- a context for learning;
- ensuring that learning objectives are clear so that children understand why they are learning what they are;
- mini-plenaries to ensure that children are refocused at various points in the lesson.

CASE STUDY - Primary - Whole School

Behaviour for Learning can be promoted on a whole-school level and, as with anything, it has a better and long-term impact when something can be implemented this way. This school developed the use of characteristics on a whole-school level.

Character Education was something that had a huge focus during the time when Justine Greening was Secretary of State for Education in the UK government, and was met with a mixture of praise and criticism.

This school took these principles and narrowed them down to key characteristics that were most important to the children. They settled on curiosity, motivation, communication, collaboration, reflection, bravery, creativity and resilience. These characteristics were embedded throughout the curriculum over a period of two years through lessons, assemblies, sports events, among many others. By making it explicitly taught and discussed on a regular basis, children became more aware of these characteristics in themselves. They were able to discuss their strengths and weaknesses when it came to these traits, working on improving their weaknesses and strengthening their strengths. This had a direct impact on children's ability to learn. Also, in turn, it reduced incidents of low-level disruption in the classroom. Children could communicate their learning explicitly and understand the process. Due to the approach of slowly embedding it over a period of two years, involving children from the point of implementation and throughout, it ensured that whole-school consistency is desirable for a stronger and long-term impact.

Behaviour can also present as a result of SEND (special educational needs and disabilities) or SEMH (social, emotional and mental health) needs. At these points, we would look at the children's main struggles, and use the support of professionals to ensure that their needs are being met properly, therefore helping to reduce problem behaviours.

A final definition of behaviour that we will discuss in this entry is extreme behaviours, also known as crisis behaviours. They can present in your classroom in different forms but will appear as heightened, manic and aggressive. Some behaviours included can be, but are not limited to, direct throwing, deliberate physical violence towards other children and/or members of your staff, direct spitting, biting, trashing of the classroom, deliberate damage to property and carrying/use of a weapon.

Extreme behaviours are typically exhibited during the flight or fight stage but, in some cases, they occur on a more regular basis. We will cover strategies that you can use in a classroom in the 'E' entry further on in this book. We will also discuss systems and processes of support, networking opportunities for support in the classroom, as well as support for those in the senior leadership team.

Must follow on Twitter:

@pmnw1 – this account is dedicated to helping young people understand the consequences of risky behaviour.

Praise Postcard

COMMUNICATION

When we are in the heat of emotion, we are so heightened that it can be difficult to communicate. Behaviour can communicate so many things within a school. It can be a cry for attention, or a way of trying to communicate emotions, among many other things, but the key to understanding it is knowing your children, knowing whether it is communication that needs to be listened to, challenged, or both, and the reasons why.

It is not only the children's communication that we need to think about. Our communication as adults in the classroom needs to be emotionally intelligent, clear and well thought through to get the desired effect of supporting children with their behaviours.

A simple, yet powerful way of adapting language in the classroom is to use positive language during interactions with children. Our language can be a supportive boundary to children when they are in 'crisis', or even when they are exhibiting low-level behaviour. You can make subtle changes to remove choice, which can be a suitable strategy for de-escalation. Here are some examples.

LOW-LEVEL BEHAVIOUR EXAMPLE

A child is fiddling with their pencil sharpener. It is causing a distraction and focusing the children away from completing their work, so you need to address it in your classroom.

Automatic reaction:

'James, please put your pencil sharpener down!'

James has the choice of putting the pencil sharpener down and carrying on with his work or of continuing to fiddle with it, which would escalate the situation.

Reducing choice provides a boundary, and limits the time taken on dealing with the behaviour.

Positive reaction:

'James, put your pencil down. Thank you.'

Choice removed. 'Thank you' clarifies that the instruction will be followed and you've still included manners for those worried that I removed the word 'please'.

EXTREME BEHAVIOUR EXAMPLE

A child is in crisis behaviour. They are indirectly throwing items around the classroom. Only you and the child are in the classroom. The child has picked up a chair.

Automatic reaction:

'Sarah, put that chair down. Don't throw that chair.'

Sarah is in crisis. To de-escalate the situation, Sarah needs support as she is in a situation where she is unable to self-regulate her emotions. The following response would give her the acknowledgement of her emotion and a way out.

Positive reaction:

In a calm voice: 'Sarah, I can see that you're angry. Put the chair down and let's walk together.'

Positive language and communication support children with a variety of different experiences, including those with attachment issues and the experience of trauma.

Table 3.1 gives some ways of changing everyday responses to positive language.

Table 3.1   Changing everyday responses to positive language

Everyday response	Positive language
Don't run inside!	Walk inside, thank you.
Don't play with the ball inside!	Take the ball outside.
Why are you so upset?	I can see that you are upset. Would you like to talk it through?
Ssssshhhhh!	Joe, you are listening well.
Could you please wait your turn to speak?	It's time to listen.

I'm sure you will feel that positive language is so simple in life, but ensuring that you are consistent with it is another thing. When dealing with behaviour, we are also in a heightened state of emotion, so unless we have practised the use of positive language, it won't be our 'go to' response.

CYBER BULLYING

There has been a steady increase over the past few years in reports of cyber bullying and how it has spilled over into schools. For school staff, it can cause great difficulty, wading in and among anonymous actions, and dealing with incidents that have started outside school. Some schools take the stance of not dealing with incidents starting outside school, but inevitably it does have consequences within the school. Educating children to be safe online and understand what they are becoming involved with needs to start at an early age, so ensuring that children are engaging in purposeful E-Safety activities in primary school is vital.

Children need to start by understanding about privacy at an early age. Passwords can be introduced as a form of log-on and can be developed into individual passwords as soon as the concept is understood. Don't shy away from this, thinking that children are too young. They will be using online websites early on, so they need to know how to keep themselves safe. In primary school, I teach my children about the 'X' in the top-right corner and always say that if they are not happy with what they are seeing, they should click the 'X' and tell an adult.

Educating parents is vital. When we have hosted sessions for parents in primary school, they have been astounded by the apps their children are on and what those apps have the capability to do. Show them how to add parental controls to their phones. One of the most successful sessions we had was a coffee morning where we asked parents to bring in their child's device and we shared how to add parental controls. It removes the fear for parents who don't feel comfortable using electronic devices.

Don't assume that children are limited to Facebook, Twitter and Instagram. They may be the most popular methods of social media for adults, but children are using a whole host more. To find out, speak to the children and they will tell you. It will help keep you updated, and you can research them for yourselves.

Cover E-Safety within Computing, of course, but it needs to spread further than that. Teach it through your Personal, Social, Health and Economic (PSHE) education.

Conduct case studies of issues you have dealt with in the past. Ask children how they would deal with these issues. Support them.

Involving your local Police Community Support Officer (PCSO) may be beneficial in the upper juniors of a primary school, but most definitely at secondary school. It allows you to add weight to the severity of the impact of social media. It can also help to educate your children on the law with social media and what their responsibilities are.

CASE STUDY - *Secondary*

A secondary school in Leicestershire found that they were having repeated incidents of cyber bullying as a result of children using social media outside school, which were having knock-on effects in school. One of the school's biggest difficulties was that the apps and sites where these incidents were occurring were ones that they hadn't experienced before. On working with the local PCSO, they decided to work on the topic by completing a simple questionnaire (see photocopiable resource). It allowed children to answer questions about the apps that they used. It enabled the school to write a scheme of work around the apps/sites that the children were using, so that they were able to support them on how to use them responsibly and with knowledge around the risks and possible consequences, rather than using them blindly.

Must follow on Twitter:

@Warning_Zone – a site dedicated to being responsible with risk taking. It also provides school visits if you are local to them. Well worth a visit with Year 6 particularly.

E-safety Questionnaire

Below is a simple questionnaire that you can complete with your children so that you can tailor your E-Safety curriculum to definitely support the learning needs of your children.

This can be completed as a paper questionnaire, but ideally you would want to use a survey site for an easier and much quicker analysis of the answers.

1. How do you access the internet?

    Phone
    Computer
    Tablet
    Other . . .

2. What apps/sites do you use that interact with other people?

    Facebook
    Twitter
    Instagram
    Snapchat
    Musical.ly
    Whatsapp
    X-Box live
    Others . . .

3. Have you ever interacted with someone online that you did not know in real life?

4. Has anyone ever said anything to you that you didn't like online?

5. If yes, did you tell anybody?

6. If no, who would you tell if someone did say something that you did not like?

7. Are your profiles set to private?

HIERARCHY
OF NEEDS

As a teacher or a member of school staff, you will have a very limited impact on a child's past. You cannot control, influence or change the first years of interaction, care and nurturing that a child receives. I completely understand how frustrating this is, considering the overwhelming influence that it has on a child's future years and, in turn, on the way that they present in school and, ultimately, your classroom.

Maslow's hierarchy of needs (see www.simplypsychology.org/maslow.html) is a very simple yet powerful theory that can be looked at alongside case studies of children within the classroom to attempt to identify possible gaps in the foundations that should have been set within early life. With this knowledge, interventions can be put in place.

The theory was presented in a triangle as a five-stage model. As a person developing, you cannot progress to the next stage without being firm in a previous stage. The first stage that Maslow presented was physiological need; the majority of children who present with behaviour difficulties do not have concrete foundations within the first few stages. To be secure within this first stage, a child must have adequate food, water, warmth, shelter, clothing and sleep.

CASE STUDY - *Primary - Jessica - Year 1*

Jessica is 5 years old and in Year 1. She is generally a happy child but struggles to settle in the mornings. Her behaviour can be unpredictable and her mood can vary, which influences the behaviour she presents. She doesn't come with a snack or water bottle and is always provided with these at school.

When looking at her case study alongside Maslow's hierarchy of needs, it is apparent that Jessica might be lacking in consistent food, nutrition and water. The school she attends has an on-site breakfast club that is a paid-for provision. The school is able to offer Jessica a funded place at breakfast club, which her family take up. Consequently, on a daily basis the first hour before school is calm for Jessica; she is able to have breakfast consistently and the breakfast club workers are able to ensure that she is calm before starting school. This has a dramatic effect on Jessica's morning stability and a positive impact on her behaviour within school.

The next stage that Maslow presented within his hierarchy of needs is the safety stage. To progress to the next stage of development, a child needs to feel secure and safe within their daily life. It is such a difficult area to be able to have consistent impact on as a school member of staff, but nevertheless you can still have that impact to support children. When a child experiences inconsistencies, it creates fear and anxiety within them synonymous with insecurity. As a consequence of this insecurity and feelings of being unsafe, behaviour difficulties present within the classroom. It is very difficult to create security and safety within a child when there is a different teacher and classroom staff on a yearly basis in a primary setting, and even more so in a secondary setting where a different face can be seen at each lesson.

CASE STUDY - *Secondary - Kamal - Year 9*

Kamal has exhibited difficult behaviours throughout his schooling. His behaviour can range from low-level disruption to impulsive behaviours to unpredictable behaviours. There appears to be no pattern to the behaviours, when they occur, where they occur and the behaviours being presented. When looking at his case study alongside Maslow's hierarchy of needs, it was apparent that Kamal lacked boundaries, consistency and a positive attachment with an adult. Kamal had many interactions with different adults during the day, all of whom would have been able to provide a positive attachment, but he was unable to form these connections.

The well-being team were focused on trying to support Kamal in feeling safe and secure. Their technique was not to focus on forming positive relationships, which might be the most common option, but by implementing the following, they were able to secure Kamal within the second phase of Maslow's hierarchy of needs, as well as helping him to enter the third. They implemented a 'meet and greet' in the morning. This was a simple technique that allowed Kamal to have a calm period of time before starting the day ahead. It was a positive interaction that allowed the team to see how Kamal's emotions were upon entering school to give them vital information on how best to support him during that day, but the key was to provide time to discuss the day ahead. This simple strategy, when completed consistently, provided Kamal with boundaries, safety and security within his day. He knew what was happening day to day. The well-being team would 'check in' during the day to avert any difficulties that he was facing and to offer support when needed. Also, when informed prior to unexpected changes, as can often occur within a school, the well-being team were able to warn Kamal about these changes to his day. The first noticeable change to Kamal's behaviour was a reduction in unexpected outbursts of behaviour and impulsivity. It took a full year of consistency in this approach for Kamal's behaviour to dramatically change, and then the well-being team were able to build on the support to lead him into the third phase.

The third phase of Maslow's hierarchy of needs is 'belongingness and love needs', where, as part of their development, children are able to develop and sustain healthy relationships. Children who are not secure within this phase can experience difficulty during breaks and lunchtimes where relationships are key and social interactions are frequent. If you have a child who is struggling with friendships, then these situations need to be worked through with a trusted adult to support children with this stage.

The next phase is 'esteem needs' where children are able to feel success and have feelings of accomplishment. Children can struggle with this and, again, may need support. Some children feel confident within this experience straight away and some need small steps and discussions.

When children have confidently progressed through these stages of development, they find themselves in the final phase: self-actualisation. Children are finally able to realise their own potential. As a teacher, this is what we crave: not to achieve the highest marks in a test or compare one child to another, but to facilitate a child to be the best that they can be.

Must follow on Twitter:

@beyondbehaviour – Steve Russell used the behaviour wall to look at these gaps in foundations; he has an interesting perspective on how teachers can support children through these phases.

Digging Down

It is important to think about a child's basic needs when you are trying to identify the areas that you need to support in order to give them the foundations for life. Use the details provided in the chapter and identify the areas that may be missing in the foundations of a child's life.

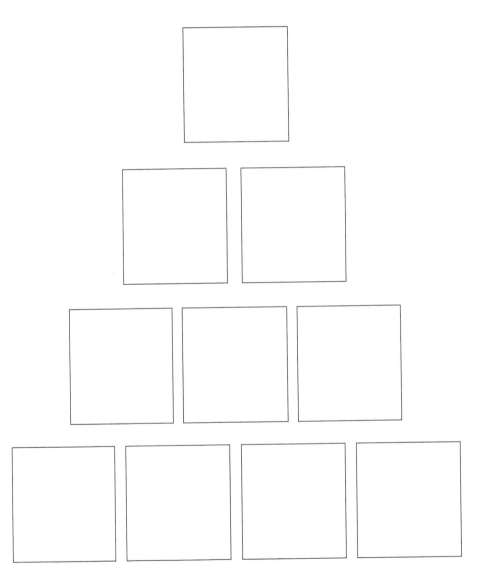

ELSA
EMOTIONAL
LITERACY
SUPPORT
ASSISTANT

It never fails to surprise me how many members of school staff have not heard of an ELSA (emotional literacy support assistant), let alone have one within school; however, it is one of the resources that can have the biggest impact. I'll be honest – it is something that I have only been exposed to within the past three years, but it is a resource that I have seen to have had the biggest impact on behaviour within my school.

WHAT IS IT?

An emotional literacy support assistant is a member of school staff designated to provide support to your vulnerable children. They are a member of school staff who needs to be trained within the ELSA programme. More information on the programme itself can be found at: www. elsanetwork.org

The person you choose to train is most likely somebody already on your school staff, so it doesn't need to be an additional position and an additional stretch on your budget. The choice of this person is key. They will be in difficult situations on a daily basis, whether it is dealing with difficult situations within school, having to deal with vulnerable families, hearing disclosures and being able to act appropriately, as well as dealing with all of these within a short day, so choose wisely. There will be minimal impact if you don't choose somebody who is able to complete the above and still have a thirst for the job.

WHAT DO THEY DO?

The job of an emotional literacy support assistant can encompass so many different strands. It can include, but is not limited to, the list below:

- Provide in-classroom support to children.
- Complete one-to-one or group sessions, in line with a block of intervention focused on the needs of children.
- Work with a variety of school staff with the key aim of providing the best support for children.
- Work with the behaviour support team and/or Special Educational Needs and Disabilities Coordinator (SENDCo) to monitor the behaviour incidents within school. This can also act as a measure of the impact of the work of an ELSA.
- Work with the families of vulnerable children. The tasks of this work can range from communicating the effectiveness of sessions with a child, to providing support for a family who may also have difficulties.
- Complete referrals to provide further support to families, as well as liaising with them to complete these referrals.
- Provide lunchtime support for those children struggling with unstructured times.
- Complete a variety of assessments to inform children's work – e.g., Boxall profiles, well-being scales, strengths and difficulties questionnaires, etc.
- Plan and provide a block of work with children. This has measurable entry and exit criteria.

WHAT SUPPORT/TRAINING DO THEY NEED?

ELSAs receive ongoing supervision, which is imperative to their continued impact. It allows them not only to refresh their training, but also to discuss those complex children who may present a variety of different behaviours. They will also have more impact within school if they are linked to the inclusion team, behaviour support team and/or SENDCo. If the SENDCo is not a member of the senior leadership team, it may also be beneficial to be linked to a member of the senior leadership team due to the strategic nature of the work that an ELSA undertakes. The senior leadership team must have an overview of the behaviour within school and a reduction in incidents that they are responsible for, so by having this relationship with these teams, there is a seamless bond within the school setting. It also supports early identification and allows direction for an ELSA's caseload. Just as a word of warning – the success of having an effective ELSA within school presents you with a new problem: many families seek the support of the ELSA, often seeing them as a solution to problems that they identify within their family life and/or their child's behaviour. The more children that an ELSA works with, the less effective they become, as they cannot have quality time to provide intervention on a regular enough basis to have an impact. I suggest that you prioritise children and be clear on the length of provision that should be undertaken.

As I mentioned before, my experience of having ELSAs in a variety of settings is successful. Below, I will share two successful examples that you may be able to identify with.

CASE STUDY – Tom – Secondary

Tom is in Year 8. His Dad passed away after a short illness, leaving him with his Mum and younger sister, Tina. In Year 7, prior to his Dad's illness, Tom presented as a confident boy who had a wide circle of friends. Following his bereavement, his persona changed and he became withdrawn. He also appeared tired and distracted. School met with Tom's Mum throughout the events as they presented and communication was good. She had taken Tom to the GP to try to seek support for him in dealing with his bereavement and they were signposted to a local bereavement charity. The counsellor reported that Tom hadn't opened up in his sessions so far. Mum was surprised by Tom's tiredness at school, and reported that he slept well and had regular bedtimes.

Mari's involvement began shortly after the death of Tom's Dad. She began with short sessions focusing on Tom's family and encouraged him to discuss his family and portray them through art activities. Within the first four weeks of short sessions, Tom began to include his Dad in conversations – e.g., 'I like fishing. My Dad used to take me.' Although it was nowhere near acknowledging the passing of his Dad, it was a start of the development of a relationship. Mari continued her work on a one-to-one basis, and collecting items that Tom mentioned in relation to his Dad – e.g., when he mentioned that his Dad was good at art, Mari put a set of watercolour paints within a memory box. After the first eight weeks of intervention, Mari discussed the memory box. Tom responded well and although tearful, was able to share memories and add to the box. This became a regular feature of their sessions. Mari then brought Mum into the sessions and Tom was able to share his memory box with her, and they began to add to it as a family. The impact on Tom was measurable. He began to talk to his Mum about his thoughts and feelings, but there was also an impact on Tom's friendship groups. His presentation gradually became similar to how he was previously and his learning levels began to improve. Mari measured her impact with a well-being scale at the beginning and end of the block of interventions. She also gained pupil voice at the end of the sessions.

CASE STUDY – Kareem – Primary

Kareem is in Year 5. Throughout his time at primary school he has struggled to control his behaviour. He presents low-level behaviour within the classroom setting, which can be managed through a variety of techniques, including silent behaviour management and positive praise. Kareem constantly wants to please and doesn't like the thought of upsetting anyone. Breaktimes and lunchtimes are the most difficult times for Kareem. He desperately wants to have a circle of friends and bonds with the other children over his love for wrestling. However, his play fighting always turns into actual fighting. Regardless of how many conflict resolution conversations are had with Kareem, these incidents are frequent. He was referred to the school's ELSA who began with some small group situations so that she could see Kareem's participation within his social group. It was during this time that she observed how he took control of the situation. She began a block of work focused on Lego therapy which looked at turn taking. Building up over the six weeks, groups went from a partnership to a group of four successfully. It was only at this point that the ELSA began one-to-one sessions, with Kareem focused on his playground behaviour. Kareem was able to identify difficulties in the playground as a barrier for him. The ELSA worked on alternative playground games and slowly brought Kareem's friendship group to the sessions to practise the games. The ELSA was also present in the playground during this intervention to support with changing Kareem's playground behaviour. Although the block of intervention was lengthy, it reduced Kareem's playground incidents to zero and he was even able to get involved with leading playground games for others.

Must follow on Twitter:

@elsasupport – contact Debbie. There are also a variety of resources that you can find at www. elsasupport.co.uk. When planning blocks of interventions, it will save you a lot of time by providing you with ready-made resources for immediate delivery.

All About Me

| The people closest to me | The things that I enjoy |

| The things that I don't like to talk about | The things that make me angry |

| The things that never fail to cheer me up |

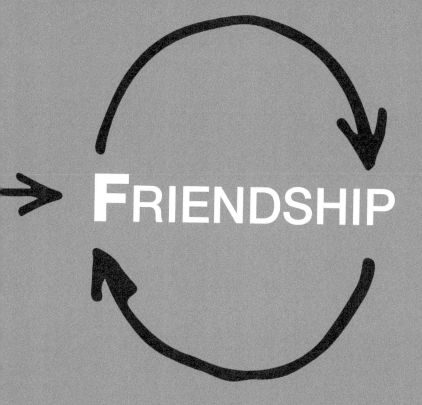

FRIENDSHIP

Friendship is often the thing that we take for granted. We teach children how to read, how to write and how to reason with their mathematics, but then we throw them into a playground with lots of other children, with no structure and limited direction, and expect everything to run smoothly – strange when you think of it, isn't it? However, if we can teach social skills and friendship from the early years, and if we continue to have this focus throughout school life, then we can support children in one of the areas that they may find the most difficult.

There are many options during a school week when you can explicitly teach these skills. Within a primary setting, they can be taught through Personal, Social, Health and Economic education (PSHE) and Citizenship, at breaktimes and at lunchtimes; however, in order for this to be successful, all school staff need to be on board. Problems may occur if children feel that they have 'no games to play' or 'no one to play with'. In primary, one strategy is to teach children some playground games and ensure that there is equipment for them to use. Children have fantastic imaginations, but can struggle when there is a lack of structure. Having a bank of games to play when their imagination struggles is ideal for a playground setting. If you can teach a couple at a time, then the bank will get bigger.

CASE STUDY - Primary School

Every school year, this primary school completes a pupil questionnaire that looks at all aspects of school life, including lunchtimes. Children reported that there wasn't anything to do at lunchtimes and that the staff didn't engage with them. The school devised a year of continuous professional development, supporting staff to learn different playground games that they could then share with the children. There was a minimal investment to buy some resources for the children, but the majority of the games were imaginative ones that children could learn to play. After a year, the school completed the same exercise of asking the children to undertake a pupil questionnaire, and 97 per cent of them said that they enjoyed the new lunchtime provision.

Here are four playground games that you can start with, and they don't require adult support once the game has been taught:

1. DUCK, DUCK, GOOSE

This is typically a game that Key Stage 1 children (ages 5–7) will enjoy, and it has no limit on how many children can play. Sit children in a circle. One child needs to be 'on'. They go round the circle, touch each child on the head saying 'duck'. They will then tag a child and say 'goose'. Upon this, the 'goose' gets up and chases the 'tagger'. If the 'tagger' gets around the circle and back into the space before getting caught, then they win and the 'goose' is 'on'. If they get caught by the 'goose', then they are 'on' again. The beauty of this game is that it burns a lot of energy, but can also be adapted based on interest. 'Duck, Duck, Goose' can be replaced by 'Cat, Cat, Dog' or even 'Luke, Luke, Yoda'.

2. HOPSCOTCH

Hopscotch is a traditional game, but unfortunately is one that few children know these days. You don't have to spend a lot of money on playground resources. All you need is a piece of chalk and a marker – e.g., a stone, button, shell, etc. for each person playing. Use chalk to draw a hopscotch pattern on the ground. This is a diagram with eight numbered sections. Each player has a marker. The first player stands behind the starting line to toss his or her marker in square one. Hop over square one to square two and then continue hopping to square eight, turn around and hop back again. Pause in square two to pick up the marker, hop in square one and out. Then continue by tossing the stone into square two. All hopping is done on one foot unless the hopscotch design is such that two squares are side by side. Then two feet can be placed down with one in each square. A player must always hop over any square where a marker has been placed. You can have the option of a player 'getting out'. A player is out if the marker fails to land in the appropriate square, if the hopper steps on a line, if the hopper loses balance when picking up the marker/puts a second hand or foot down, if the hopper goes into a square where a marker is, or if a player puts two feet down in a single box.

3. WHAT'S THE TIME, MR WOLF?

This game does not require any additional playground equipment, nor does it have a cap on numbers. One child acts as 'Mr Wolf' and stands at the front facing away from the other children. The other children stand at the other end of the playground. They all chorus and shout 'What's the time, Mr Wolf?'. The wolf shouts a number between 1 and 12 o'clock – e.g., 3 o'clock. Whatever the number, the children take this amount of steps forward – e.g., three steps. This continues until the children get close to 'Mr Wolf'. When 'Mr Wolf' thinks the children are close, he waits for them to shout 'What's the time, Mr Wolf?' and then he shouts 'Dinner time!', turns around and chases the children. If he tags a child before they get back to the beginning, then that person is 'on'. If he doesn't catch any children, he is 'Mr Wolf' again.

4. STUCK IN THE MUD

This game does not require any additional playground equipment, nor does it have any cap on numbers. One child is 'on'. They chase all the other children around the playground. Once they tag a child, they have to stand still with their arms and legs stretched apart. To be released, one of the children who hasn't been caught has to either run under the arm of the child who has been tagged or crawl in between their legs. Once this has been completed, the child who had previously been caught is free to run again. The game only ends when all the children have been tagged and are all 'stuck in the mud'.

The beauty of knowing so many games for the playground is that it adds structure to a time that doesn't even appear like structure. As children become more confident in the playground, they can take up roles such as play leader or mentor, supporting children who struggle more with the concept of playground and friendships. Sometimes a child may require an intervention when they continue to struggle, but the most important part is that children *do* need to be taught these social skills, and this should not be overlooked.

For more ideas and information, please see: www.bl.uk/playtimes

Must follow on Twitter:

@JennyMosleyQCT – Jenny has written many books on playground games and often shares insightful tweets on supporting friendships within school.

What Makes a Good Friend?

Fill the space with qualities that you feel make a 'good friend'. To challenge a child even further, do *they* exhibit these behaviours or traits?

GREEN
(REWARDS AND
COMPENSATION)

Green seems to be that universal symbol that all is going well. We see green on a traffic light and it symbolises 'go'; it equates to good behaviour and various 'going for green' reward schemes.

In life, there are rewards and consequences. You get up in the morning and go to work. You get paid to do so (reward) and if you do something wrong, then you are spoken to (consequence). I appreciate I am being very simplistic in this, but it is true. Children are the same. In their school life, there are rewards and consequences. This gives a basic structure and set of boundaries for children in the daily life of school.

Children will respond to the rewards and consequences within your school in the first instance if they are clearly presented. The best way of starting a new school year is to go through your behaviour policy. Second, they will respond if everybody is consistent with these sets of rewards and consequences. This can be quite tricky because of the age-old debate around extrinsic and intrinsic rewards. Extrinsic rewards are usually financial or something material. They are external to the school. Other people decide what they are and whether or not they are granted. Intrinsic motivation refers to children exhibiting positive behaviour that is driven by internal processes and internal rewards. It originates from within the children themselves. It is really important to be clear on your rewards, because if you use extrinsic rewards, then children can become dependent on them. There are a variety of different rewards that can be effective for children.

INDIVIDUAL REWARDS

When I think of individual rewards, I think of children who may be on a behaviour plan and who have those motivators to support their progress. However, this isn't always the case. Individual rewards can be for everyone.

Primary

1. Body language – children can be praised through smiles and thumbs-up for recognition of what they are doing well. This doesn't have to be just in the classroom. It can be walking through the corridor and passing a child who is walking calmly and simply smiling at them. It is an acknowledgment that they are exhibiting the appropriate behaviours.
2. Stickers/stampers – stickers and stampers have caused quite a debate in terms of them being viewed as extrinsic rewards and children behaving in order to receive them. However, they do provide an individual reward that children can work towards. They also serve as a reminder to the child of something that they have done well during that day.
3. Sticker charts – again, they can cause a debate, but they are a great way for children to see their successes during the day. They will look different for each child, as they will tie in to any behaviour plans that have been created for each individual. The stickers themselves can act as the reward, or you may want to have a reward at the end of the day or week, such as 15 minutes of quiet reading or 15 minutes choosing activities.

Secondary

It is important to have age-appropriate rewards. However, the strategies above can be used for some secondary children. In addition, there are other options for rewards:

1. Postcards home – these can be an excellent way of celebrating successes with behaviour with those at home. The children don't know that the postcards are being sent to their home, which makes it a nice surprise when they are received. Postage will incur additional cost, so some schools send them home with the child. This does remove the surprise and the guarantee that it will make it home; however, budget may limit you.

2. Phone calls home – again, this is an excellent way of celebrating successes with behaviour with those at home. One of the strengths of this reward is that you can also have a conversation and check in with someone at home. Another benefit is that you can talk to the child and ask who they would like you to call. It makes the reward more personal to that individual.

CLASS REWARDS

Due to the amount of movement during the school day, this is more applicable to those in a primary setting. It is nice to have an individual approach to a class reward system. I have seen many versions of class rewards, but they all include working towards a goal. The best approach is to decide on a reward as a class, such as 15 minutes of extra play, additional computing time, etc. When a class decides on a reward together, it is more powerful in bringing peers together towards a common goal. Some classes collect marbles in a jar and some collect stars on a chart, but the premise is the same.

WHOLE-SCHOOL REWARDS

Many schools now operate some version of a house system, where children receive individual rewards – e.g., house points that are collected alongside others to compete against the other houses to win a reward. You can link a variety of different school events to houses as well. Secondary schools compete in house competitions and primary schools usually compete within their houses on their sports days.

Secondary

Some examples of whole-school rewards are as follows:

1. End-of-year reward trip – children can accumulate merit stickers or house points to achieve a specific total, allowing them to be involved in the end-of-year reward trip.

2. Oscars Awards Ceremony – this is a fantastic way of celebrating the achievements of individuals on a larger basis. Children are recognised for different subjects, and for demonstrating the values of the school.

CASE STUDY – *Secondary*

With rewards systems there is always the argument that the children who behave don't receive rewards. This is not my argument, but it is one that I've heard many times. To combat this, the school implemented the end-of-year reward trip. Children have to receive 100 stamps to be able to attend the trip. It allows children's success to be rewarded and celebrated. It also gives the children something to aspire to year on year. It was reported that parents were happy with this addition to the rewards system and that the children felt they had something they needed to work towards through fear of missing out.

As with anything, rewards can have an excellent impact on children's behaviour when they are used consistently and when they are genuine. Extrinsic rewards do have their place, but it is important to have a clear strategy around intrinsic rewards in order to build that sense of personal achievement into the behaviour.

Must follow on Twitter:

@classdojo – an online resource that allows children to accumulate points when they show positive behaviour. It can be used in a variety of different ways, depending on the needs of your setting and children.

Reward Another

This reward option goes one step forward and rewards another. Ask the children to think about someone who has done something for them and to complete the activity with that in mind. It doesn't have to be something that you share, but can just be a source of reflection.

Admit One

Admit One

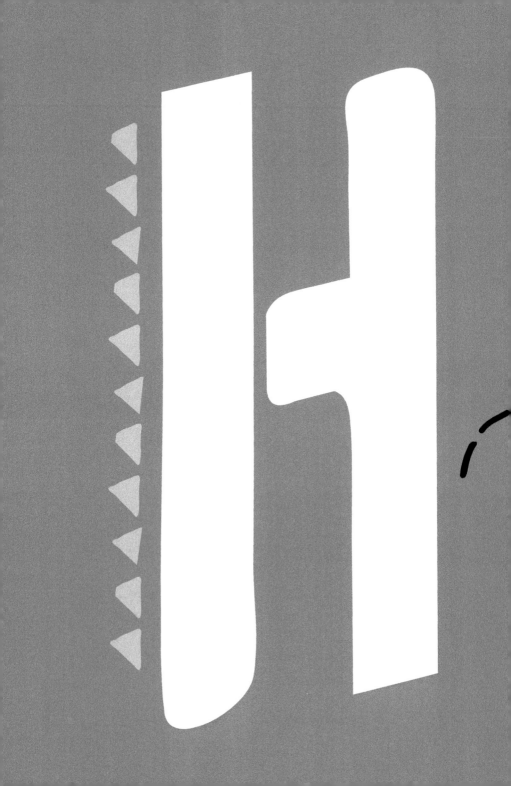

I
NEED
HELP!

Let's start with something that every reader should know: nobody in a classroom should ever be left to deal with any behaviours without the support of others. I would hope that you are in a supportive environment where you can discuss the behaviours that everybody faces in the classroom without fear or judgement. However, this entry is designed to be that support, which may or may not be present in your school.

One of the first things that I suggest you do if you are beginning to feel that behaviour is becoming difficult to manage, is to look at your whole-school behaviour policy. I realise this may seem like a simple suggestion, but it can be very powerful to strip behaviour right back to the basics. As a member of school staff, it isn't unreasonable to expect to be supported by an effective behaviour policy; this needs to be reviewed on a regular basis, to ensure that it is fit for purpose and effectively supporting school staff in dealing with daily behaviours. If this isn't the case, then suggest a review with your line manager. It might be that other school staff are in the same position. This will be even more powerful if you are able to take some suggestions for amendments to the meeting. Sometimes when behaviour has been tricky and demanding, you may be in a position where you cannot think clearly about any amendments that may support you further. If this is the case, then spend some time gauging opinion from school staff. If it's one particular set of students that you see once a week, then discuss it with other members of staff who work with them as well. If it is a class that you teach on a daily basis, then speak to the classroom staff who work with them on a daily basis: teaching assistants, learning mentors, sports coaches or behaviour mentors. Even just in these two scenarios there is a plethora of expertise that you can tap into for ideas for amendments that you could take forward to a review meeting.

On the other hand, it could be that you do feel supported by a behaviour policy, but you are encountering behaviour that still requires additional support. It's at this point that I feel I must say that talking about behaviour is not a weakness. If somebody makes you feel it is a weakness, then it is their weakness, not yours. Regardless of your position in school and/or years that you have worked in education, behaviour is challenging for all school staff. School staff may not find the same child as challenging, or be struggling with behaviour at the same time, but all school staff will find difficulties with behaviour at some time, so rest assured, by being proactive and reading this book, you are not weak. You will find strength and continue to be a strong practitioner. Below are two case studies that you may be able to identify with if you have encountered behaviour that is not supported by an effective behaviour policy.

CASE STUDY - Jenny - Secondary

Jenny is a Year 7 girl. She arrived from one of the feeder primaries. During transition meetings, you were provided with the information that Jenny is vulnerable and that she has had extensive support from the ELSA (emotional literacy support assistant). You have been teaching her for an hour a day for English. She presents as a disorganised student, who regularly arrives late to your lesson and in a fluster. She finds it very hard to settle down, often disrupting others during your lesson. On regular occasions she refuses to complete tasks you set. When she does attempt a task, it appears that she does it without any effort and it is not to your expectations. You have used your school's behaviour policy, but this often results in calling the 'on duty' member of the School Leadership Team (SLT) and removing Jenny from the classroom. Despite this being a regular consequence for Jenny, you are not seeing any improvement in her behaviour. This is also having an effect on the teaching input that other children in the class are receiving.

Here are two options that you may want to consider:

1. Speak to your behaviour team and raise a cause for concern. They will be able to support Jenny with her transition into class. By arriving on time, it may reduce her anxiety/disorganisation. A behaviour mentor will not only be able to support Jenny in this, but also support her to settle and be prepared for your input. There is also the option that a member of the behaviour team may be able to 'check in' during the tasks, to ensure that she is working with high expectations. Encouragement from them may be available as additional support in class, and allow you to teach without disruptions. With the additional support, a relationship may well develop between Jenny and the behaviour mentor which would allow further support throughout Jenny's time at secondary school.

2. Arrange a meeting between the team in Jenny's primary school and yourself/behaviour team. It should be noted that although the settings are very different, there is something that they both have in common: Jenny. Between the two teams, there will be strategies that will enable her to be successful within school and your lessons. By having both settings there, you are also creating a support network for yourself.

CASE STUDY – *Leila – Primary*

Leila has been in your primary school since Reception (ages 4–5). She is now in Year 3 (ages 7–8). She demonstrates difficult behaviours, whether it is causing disruption in the classroom and/or having friendship difficulties. Despite consequences for her behaviour in line with your whole-school behaviour policy, there has been no improvement in Leila's behaviour, which has declined since the beginning of her time at your primary school. Her parents have engaged when you have spoken to them, and they are keen to do anything they can to support their daughter's behaviour.

Here are two options that you may want to consider:

1. Just as you could with Jenny, arrange a meeting with all staff involved with Leila including the school ELSA. We mentioned that Leila's parents are supportive, so it may be beneficial to invite Leila's parents to the meeting. This meeting is designed to gain a whole view of the way Leila presents in every aspect of her life. Start by discussing how Leila presents at home. What are her strengths? Are there any difficulties in behaviour? Then continue the meeting by thinking about how Leila presents as a friend. Are there any areas in which the friendship difficulties arise more than others? Have the parents seen these difficulties arise at their home with friends? At parties? Finally, move on to how Leila presents in school. Round off the meeting by discussing commonalities in the presentations in different areas. Are there huge differences? You will find the meeting really does give you a fuller and clearer picture of Leila as an individual.

2. Complete a Boxall Profile assessment of Leila. Sometimes when the behaviour is varied, it can be hard to pinpoint the areas to support. A Boxall Profile is a framework for assessing children and young people who have social, emotional and behavioural difficulties and are failing at school. It has a diagnostic and developmental focus, and it will help you to identify the areas where the child needs the most support. It doesn't mean that all the other areas are not important, nor does it mean that you will see instant results, but it does mean that you are more likely to provide support that will have a long-term impact on Leila's behaviour and engagement with school.

The strategies in both the primary and secondary case studies are not exclusive to each setting. There are also other options that you can explore in your local area. Behaviour panels are set up in the local area and you may find these within your local authority, Family of School, Teaching School Alliance and/or Multi-Academy Trust. They are designed to be non-threatening opportunities for you to discuss the child with whom you are finding difficulties. Typically, a session runs as follows:

- Meetings are made up of members of school staff, such as head teachers, teachers, support staff, behaviour mentors, specialists, etc.
- People present their case studies and you will be directed as to when it is your turn.
- You will present your child's situation, and give as much detail as you can and include any actions you are taking and strategies that you have tried with the impact that they are having. This will allow for people to give effective strategies rather than repeating anything that you have already tried.
- Members of the panel will provide strategies that you may not have tried. They may also signpost you to support services in your local area.

Allowing for local differences, depending on where you are teaching, there will still ultimately be some support for you from these meetings and you will widen your network.

Another option for you as a member of school staff is to contact the local alternative provision. In the majority of cases, if you want support in your sessions or classroom, there is the option to 'buy in' support from your local alternative provision. There is usually a cost and with budgets always being quite tight, this may not be an option. If it is an option, not only will it provide effective support to the child, but it will also be an effective form of continuing professional development (CPD) for you and your school staff. If it is not an option, then there is usually a telephone service that will allow you to gain expertise from specialists in behaviour. Personally, I have sought support with a variety of children from our local alternative provision to the point where I have an excellent relationship with the staff. I cannot recommend this highly enough. There is always a strategy that I have not thought of, or a new assessment that I can use within my classroom, so pick up the phone and try your local alternative provision.

I'll start with exactly the same message as I began with. This entry is entitled 'I need help' for a very simple reason. Everybody needs support with behaviour at regular points of their career. You won't be the first to seek that support, and you certainly won't be the last. It is not a weakness. It is a strength and a sign of how much of a reflective practitioner you are. For further support, join in with my weekly Twitter chat on Mondays (during term time) from 8pm to seek instantaneous support from a variety of people nationwide. I'm sure you will be able to support others as well.

For detailed information on the Boxhall Profile and how it works, visit the website at: https://boxallprofile.org

Must follow on Twitter:

Follow me at **@behaviourteach** or tag #behaviourchat to access further, free CPD or ask practitioners to support you in finding solutions or strategies to move forward.

Diamond 9

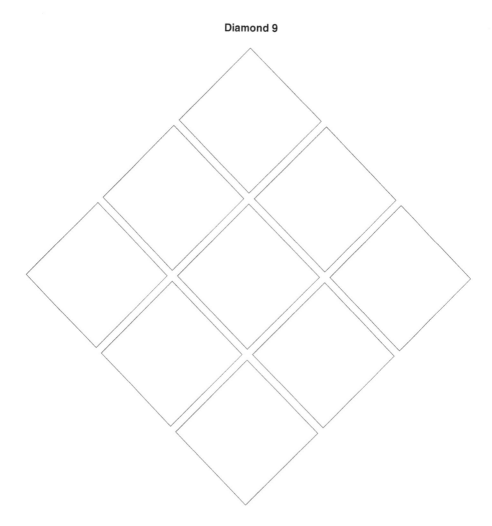

When networking with someone, you want to keep the perspective of the issue. If you are discussing the behaviour of a particular child, then use the resource above to give a type of priority to the behaviours. At the top, write the behaviour that you find the most difficult to deal with, then continue until you have either completed the diamond 9 or run out of behaviours.

This will focus your conversation and you are more likely to discuss strategies that will have a direct impact on the behaviours within your classroom.

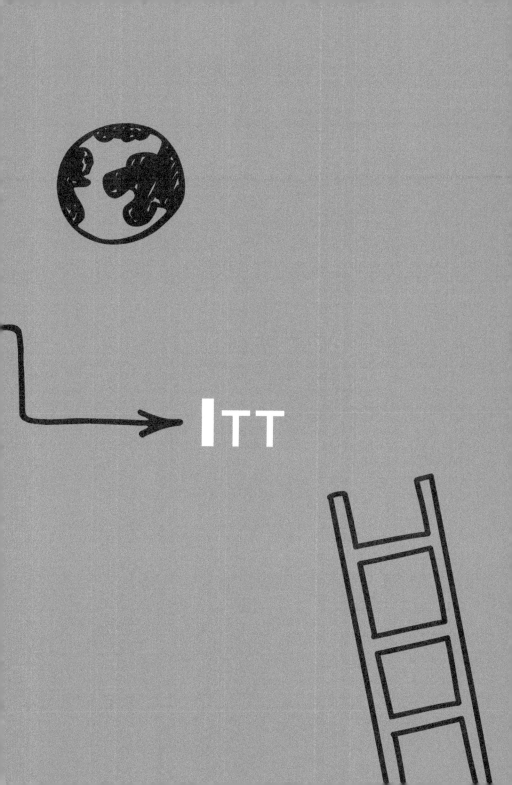

ITT

You're lucky if you get more than two sessions on behaviour management in your training year, and are then expected to be able to work with the behaviour of an individual, group, whole class and whole school. Please do not misunderstand me – this is by no means the fault of any ITT provider. I am merely trying to make the point that if we don't continue to discuss behaviour during our careers, then skills will never deepen or move forward.

PRE-PLACEMENT

To be well informed prior to placement is to be well prepared. As soon as you know the school in which you will be completing your placement, begin the research. Use the school website or speak to your link mentor/school member of staff in order to obtain whole-school policies, including the behaviour policy. Read through the behaviour policy and take note of the systems and processes that are in place to support you. When you are clear on what these are and how you think they will look within your school day, then prepare any questions you have or any further points/thoughts that you need clarifying. Another key action for you to complete prior to starting your placement is to get a staff list. You need to know who is responsible for behaviour, the clear communication chain within your department or Key Stage and who is the Special Educational Needs and Disabilities Co-ordinator (SENDCo).

ON PLACEMENT OR ON THE JOB

For the first day of your placement and/or new job, take your points and/or thoughts that you want clarified and identify the best person with whom to discuss the behaviour policy. Ask this person how the behaviour policy looks in a classroom on a whole-school level. If you simply read through the policy or just talk to someone about the policy in the classroom, there is room for misinterpretation or inconsistency. It is important to do both and spend some time discussing it. There are strategies that are important to employ during placements in your training, as well as when starting a new job, regardless of how many years you have been teaching:

1. Learn names – the sooner that you learn names, the easier it becomes to start relationships, and we know how important it is to have a relationship with the children when working with behaviour.

2. Get to know your children – ask about and understand the individual needs of your children, so that you know how they like their achievements celebrated and what their trigger points are.

CASE STUDY - Primary

During my teacher training year, on one placement I taught a class where the majority of children had social, emotional and mental health difficulties. Bearing in mind that placements are a matter of weeks and that relationships are difficult to build up within that short space of time, I had to focus. I made it my mission to get to know each and every child in that class and to share their achievements with them. I was able to identify how best to support each child with the support of my very effective mentor, with the result that I was able to make progress with them, even in that short space of time. In fact, this was the point at which I fell in love with supporting children with additional needs.

3. Use seating plans – when knowing the individual needs of your children, plan your seating plan accordingly so that you can put children together who bring out the potential in each other, or separate personalities where needed. In a primary setting, it is important to think through these individual needs for places where you need to line up – e.g., for breaktimes, lunchtimes and assemblies.

4. Plan accordingly – once steps 2 and 3 are complete, you can think through how best you can teach to inspire all children. Although we differentiate for every different subject, we stumble over differentiating for behaviour, yet this can be the lynchpin of success.

5. Have a bank of strategies – think about your knowledge of behaviour strategies as a toolkit. Learn and research different strategies to add to the toolkit. You won't need to use all your strategies at once – some you won't need to use for years, but others you may use more frequently. The most common strategies you will need will be for low-level behaviour. Turn to the 'L' entry to find some strategies to add to your toolkit.

6. Evaluate these strategies – difficulties can arise when you apply strategy after strategy without evaluating effectiveness, so reflect on what works well as part of that strategy and discuss it with others. Make sure that this is key to your working. Implement a strategy and give it time to embed, but make regular evaluations with colleagues before determining its effectiveness.

7. Relationships – develop professional relationships with other colleagues. In order to have the most success with behaviour within your school, you will need others. To work your way through different scenarios, you will need to talk these through with others. No matter how experienced you are, this is one of the biggest strengths cited by teachers and school staff. This is a two-way experience and colleagues will look to you to discuss scenarios and/or difficulties with, so please ensure you're available to support others as much as you seek support.

During your training year, you are likely to experience feeling overloaded. Behaviour can push this to the edge, as it is so fuelled with emotion. Remember, however, that your training year is viewed as one of the hardest of your career, so keep perspective, keep focused and keep pushing forward. Good luck!

Must follow on Twitter:

@jonreidobu – Jon Reid works at Oxford Brookes University training teachers and is full of tips throughout the year.

@ILSCITT – an outstanding teacher-training provider in Leicestershire who tweets regularly throughout the year to support those in their training year.

Me and You

In order to get a basis for developing relationships, use this simple activity to help you get to know each other.

Three things you like:

_____

_____

_____

_____

_____

_____

Three things your adult likes:

_____

_____

_____

_____

_____

_____

Discussion point:

- Are there any similarities?
- What are the differences?

This will give you a basis for discussion during the days.

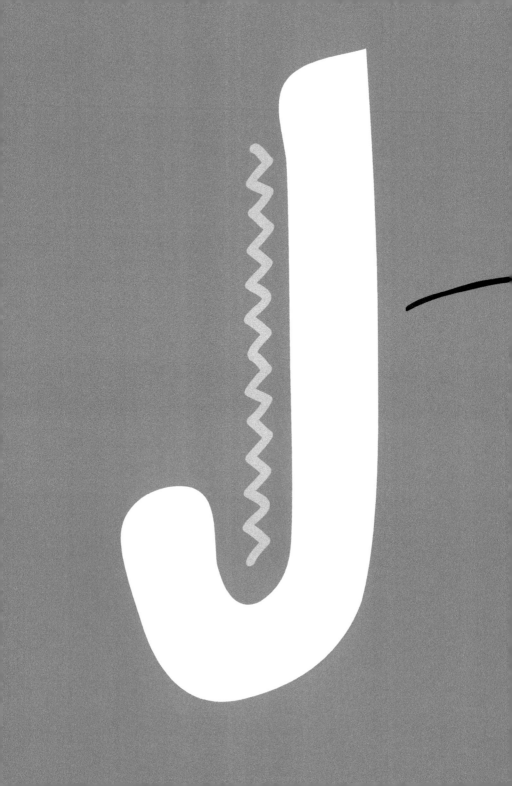

JIGSAW

Children are complex. I'm sure you may have chuckled as you read that. I did too, in the knowledge that just when you think you've figured them out, they blindside you with some new information. In order to understand a child as much as you can, you must look at the whole child, and this chapter will support you to do so. When you have a child exhibiting difficult behaviours, it really can seem rather overwhelming to the point of not being able to see through the muddy waters to get to the other side. To get some clarity, it would be helpful to break down behaviour into manageable chunks. I appreciate that this is easier said than done, but if you simply add some systems to the way you think about a situation, then it will provide a scaffold to help you to move forward with a purpose.

CASE STUDY - Primary - Mahmood - Aged 4

Mahmood presents as a happy and lively boy. Prior to coming to school, he had attended nursery part-time and it was reported that he enjoyed construction and small-world play. Mum and Dad met with the school SENDCo prior to their son starting school as there were concerns over speech and language needs. Dad in particular was concerned that Mahmood appeared so far behind other children of a similar age on the street on which he lived. When starting school, Mahmood was noticeably behind in his reading, writing and maths. His speech and language were also way behind his peers. However, the area that was most noticeably different from others was his behaviour. He didn't follow any of the school rules and engaged in physical play. His teacher struggled, particularly because there didn't seem to be a trigger to his behaviour. He was popular with his peers and the only time he hurt others was when the physical play became too rough. It is important to note that these occasions were not one-sided. Mahmood was difficult to understand, just as he was very eager to please. All parties involved were concerned, so met to look at the situation as it was becoming incredibly overwhelming for all relevant parties. They used the following framework, which supported the group to reflect on the situation and assess which areas they could support Mahmood with to improve the situation. (See the photocopiable resource at the end of the chapter.)

When the group sat together and analysed Mahmood's areas of difficulty, the first place that they all noticed were his speech and language needs. They analysed the intervention that they had completed and noted that he had made limited progress. They referred Mahmood to a speech and language therapist who was able to support his development, which showed that he had a real delay. After six months of support, Mahmood began to make some progress with his speech and language, but this didn't have any impact on his learning, so the group went back to the speech and language therapist, who was able to advise on support for his learning.

After another six months, Mahmood continued to make further progress. This began to have some impact on his behaviour. Although he still continued to want to engage in physical play, despite this being against lunchtime rules, he began to follow simple rules within the classroom. By using the progress form (provided at the end of this entry), the behaviour felt less overwhelming, and everyone involved felt there was more of a structure and process to supporting him.

CASE STUDY - Secondary - Carla - aged 11

Carla presents as a withdrawn child who doesn't engage with adults in her school. She does appear to have friendships, but these friendships would not be classed as strong bonds. Carla lives with her Dad and some younger siblings. She often arrives late, but no more than 30 minutes late. School have contacted her Dad for meetings about Carla's attendance. He always agrees to come, but does not attend meetings and always has an excuse why he cannot attend.

When questioned within class, Carla shows potential within her subjects, but she doesn't bring in homework or coursework, so her predicted grades are lower than they should be. She doesn't show a desire to learn or an interest in anything but talking to friends. When asked about future aspirations, Carla says she doesn't have any, nor does she want to think about future careers. Although Carla's behaviour is not classed as extreme, those adults around her are worried. The attendance team are concerned and feel that Carla may be acting as a caregiver at home, although they do not have definitive proof. Carla's teachers are concerned that she is not reaching her full potential. They get together to use the above framework and discuss concerns. The well-being team are invited for their input. The first area of difficulty is Carla's lateness. They decide to complete the following actions:

- Attendance officer and a member of the well-being team to visit Dad at home and discuss a referral to Strengthening Families.
- Refer to Strengthening Families.

When they attend the home, Carla's Dad discusses the difficulties he is facing at home in caring for the younger siblings. Although Carla is not providing daily childcare for the siblings, she does support her Dad. He accepts the referral to Strengthening Families and receives support from a local support worker. Over the next eight months, the support worker helps Carla's Dad with aspects of home life. When the group get back together to evaluate the actions completed, they note that Carla's lateness has improved, and consequently there is an improvement in her engagement within school. Dad's relationship with school has also improved, and he has now engaged with adult learning to support Carla with her schoolwork, which is the next focus for the team.

Must follow on Twitter:

@VPDearne – Mark Allen tweets regularly on how to support behaviour in secondary school.

Progress Form

Name:	Date: *(this is important so that you can review progress)*	
Areas of difficulty:		
List areas of difficulty in each square but start with the area of difficulty that you noticed first		
Actions: *No more than five and start with the first area of difficulty*		
Impact: *List three successes*		

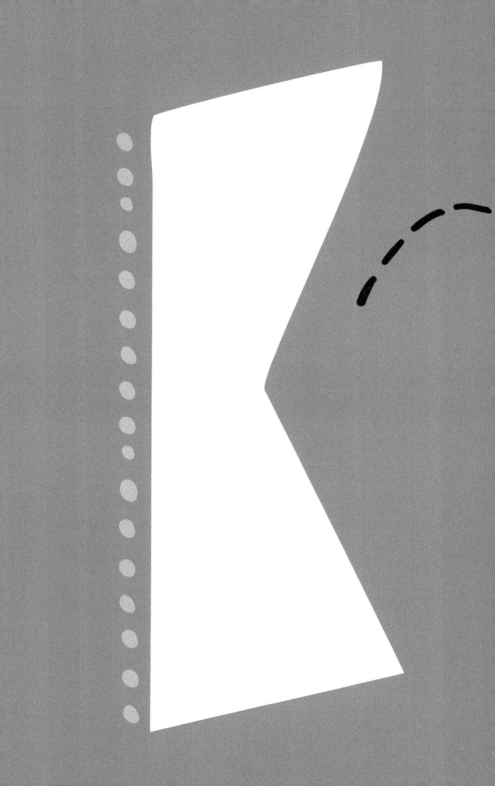

KNOWLEDGE

As a profession, we always seek solutions to problems. Low budgets? We look for a solution. A lesson goes wrong? We look for a solution. Difficult behaviour? We look for a solution. The knowledge we gain from a continued interest in behaviour is invaluable. A basic knowledge of theories around behaviour is not only interesting, but also fundamental to the understanding of it, and this chapter could be thousands of words long. There are so many books on theories of behaviour. I will keep the theories short and sweet, and focus on those that are most well known and useful to the classroom. By understanding these theories, school staff can define their individual classroom management and make informed decisions around how best to approach situations and interact with children.

B.F. SKINNER – CONTRIBUTION TO LEARNING THEORY

Although B.F. Skinner's theory (Skinner, 1953) was shared in the 1960s, it really does remain relevant to today's classroom, as it ties in not only with changing behaviour, but also with the rewards and consequences that are prevalent in the classroom. Skinner's research claims that changes in behaviour are a result of a child's response to events in life or stimuli that occur in their environment. He feels that when a specific behavioural pattern is rewarded, the child is conditioned to respond in a similar way in the future. Skinner's theories were not just for children, but I am discussing them here in the context of children's behaviour.

The key point to Skinner's theory, which was based on his own research, is that reinforcement strengthens the response received. When looking at a classroom and reward system, this is exactly what we expect from our rewards when they are given, whether intrinsic or extrinsic. Skinner made it clear that reinforcement included intrinsic or extrinsic rewards, whether it was praise, achieving an expected grade or a feeling of achievement. Many schools have a reward system that is influenced by Skinner's theory, whether it is intended or not. Teachers use immediate praise; they feed back to children and they use immediate rewards in a systematic way when trying to modify unwanted behaviours that children exhibit.

GLASSER'S CHOICE THEORY

William Glasser's theory (Glasser, 1998) generally suggests that all we do is behave. He suggests that almost all behaviour is chosen, but we are driven by genetics to satisfy the five basic needs, which he suggests are: survival, love and belonging, power, fun and freedom. Glasser states that the most important need is love and belonging, as he felt that by being connected to others, the basics are there to support a child in their ability to satisfy all other needs. He suggests that, with this in mind, the classroom should therefore be a needs-satisfying place for children. Glasser talks about teachers as managers who need to be effective in their management of a classroom, in order to be successful as teachers. He discusses the role of the teacher and says that they need to guide children in understanding that working hard and being obedient are imperative to success. Glasser states that teachers can achieve this through developing positive and strong relationships with children. He does not believe in using rewards, as he feels that these act as coercion. He believes that teachers should build these positive relationships with children and 'manage' them that way.

Glasser encourages teachers to expect the utmost best. Children should always exhibit competence and high-quality work each and every time. He also talks about self-evaluation. Teachers are expected to guide children with their behaviour, but he says that children should take ownership of their own behaviour, evaluate it and continually move forward. He feels that if a teacher manages a child in this way, they will be responsible, set and reach their own goals, become skilled in decision-making and be actively involved in improving their own behaviour.

KOHN'S STUDENT-DIRECTED LEARNING THEORY

Kohn's theory is even more recent (Kohn, 2006). He is critical of many aspects of traditional education, but specifically critiques the use of competition or external factors that motivate changes in behaviour. His thoughts are that they become inefficient over a period of time. He argues that positive reinforcement encourages attention-seeking behaviour, and that children are more likely to seek out more positive reinforcements than to actually complete their learning. Kohn believed that the most effective classroom encourages curiosity and cooperation. He believes that there should not be a strict curriculum or homework, but that a child's curiosity should be at the heart of learning. He suggests that teachers who promote cooperation and fulfil curiosity will have a classroom with positive behaviour. Kohn recognises that classrooms will be lively and full of learning, but states that behaviour management will not be needed, nor will reward systems or consequences. You may find that Kohn's theories are more likely to feature in an early years classroom or a nursery setting.

Some settings are based around learning theories, and individual practice may reflect some of the learning experiences.

CASE STUDY – Primary School

Juno Primary School employs the key messages from Skinner's theory of positive reinforcement. There are clear rewards for positive behaviour and these are designed to reinforce desired behaviours. The school saw a reduction in behavioural incidents, as well as increasing the independence of children in terms of their ability to resolve conflicts with each other.

After reading these theories, I'm sure you will agree that it is interesting to see how these theories fit into daily practice and daily life in a primary or secondary school. Reflect on these theories and see which one features most heavily in your school and your classroom. Do you think you might make some changes to your own routines after reading about the different theories and approaches?

Must follow on Twitter:

@**butterflycolour** – works daily with behaviour and SEND. Anita Devi is very approachable and keen to work in collaboration with others to improve outcomes for young people.

REFERENCES

Glasser, W. (1998) *Choice Theory: A New Psychology of Personal Freedom*. New York: Harper Perennial.

Kohn, A. (2006) *Beyond Discipline: From Compliance to Community*. Alexandria, VA: Association for Supervision and Curriculum Development.

Skinner, B.F. (1953) *Science and Human Behaviour*. New York: Free Press.

Theories

Key points to take from a theory

What can you take to put straight into your classroom?

LOW-LEVEL DISRUPTION

When you talk to people in education, low-level disruption is one of the biggest challenges that teachers face on a daily basis. As with any area of behaviour, there really is no magic wand and low-level disruption is seen as a big challenge because it appears in very different ways in very different settings and contexts. Because of this, the entry will be split into different sections. It will provide you with some ideas and strategies to use in a primary or a secondary setting, as well as giving you a brief checklist if you are in a rush and need some quick wins.

ASSEMBLIES

Your classroom management of low-level disruption is one thing, assemblies are another. You go from managing approximately 30 children to having to manage hundreds or thousands of children, where you may not have the individual relationships that we have talked about in other parts of the book. Try the following checklist:

- Staff to reinforce expectations before leaving classrooms about noise, behaviour, etc.
- Staff to present on the doors at the entry to the assembly to reinforce expectation and positive behaviour.
- Give a thought or discussion point upon entry to engage children straight away.
- Plan the assembly as if you were planning a lesson. Keep it engaging and ensure that your point/purpose of the assembly is clear.
- Ensure that your expectations are clear throughout the assembly and make sure that staff continue to reinforce these expectations.

TRANSITIONS

You know that you have effective whole-school behaviour when children behave properly when no one is looking. Transitions are one of the last things you have to tie up to really ensure that you have high expectations with behaviour. All staff need to be focused on behaviour at all points, at all times, and we all know how draining this can be to stay on the top of your game all the time. However, it *does* get easier as expectations are cemented and, before long, all you will need to do is spot the positive behaviour. Try the following ideas:

- Use positive language when you want to correct inappropriate behaviour – e.g., 'Walk, thank you', instead of 'Stop running!'.
- **Challenge poor behaviour, even if it is a child whose name you do not know or with whom** you have no relationship.
- Praise behaviour, even if it is a child whose name you don't know or with whom you have no relationship.
- Share the positivity – talk to other children about the great behaviours you have seen.

CASE STUDY - Secondary

Transitions in primary can be difficult, but in secondary they are continuous throughout the day. Children are required to transition between each lesson, which is a huge change from primary. To support this from the very beginning, the school in this case study had high visibility from staff during these times. The Pastoral Team had worked alongside the feeder primaries to identify those children who would struggle during this time, and assigned them a mentor from Year 11 to support them during these times for the first half-term. These actions supported a smooth transition and a successful move into secondary school.

NOISY SUBJECTS

I appreciate there is a place for noise during lessons, but I'm talking about those lively lessons where behaviour could easily overtake the actual learning, such as PE, computing, music, etc. They are the lessons that you just dread to be observed teaching, for the above reasons. However, if you can add some structure to the lesson, then you will channel the learning, and you should be able to avoid challenging behaviour and facilitate some fantastic sessions. Until behaviour expectations are clear and followed, the following strategies will support you in achieving your aim:

* Structure your lessons so that you share the learning as you would in your own classroom. Children need to focus, just as they would for your input in a classroom.
* Have clear rules on using equipment. These need to be followed first time and every time. If they aren't, then remove the piece of equipment. I appreciate that this may seem harsh, but it works. As soon as children realise that your boundaries are clear, in place and non-negotiable, they will use the equipment with respect and within expectations. When establishing clear rules for using equipment, include discussion about how important it is to respect equipment, that it is a resource that costs the school money and that it cannot be easily replenished. Share why it is down to everybody to ensure that the equipment is in good condition for everybody to use.
* Mini-plenaries – these will really support your sessions, not simply to refocus the learning but also to refocus the energy, attention and behaviour. It is a positive strategy that prevents you from having to use consequences in a session. It pre-empts any difficulties and is a proactive strategy in keeping a positive and enjoyable lesson.

CALLING OUT

Calling out can be incredibly frustrating for the children in your class and for you if you are trying to assess someone else's understanding of a topic or a question. It could also have a positive side, as the child calling out may be simply totally enthralled by the learning and be very eager to show this. Calling out needs to be minimised, as it detracts from what you are trying to do in your classroom, which is to provide learning for all, not one. There are many strategies that you can employ to minimise this disruption and the following are some ideas:

* Use your presence – if someone is continually calling out, then you can walk around your classroom and place yourself close to the child who is being disruptive. This is usually enough to refocus attention or give non-verbal clues to a child to indicate that their behaviour is not showing you they are engaging, and furthermore it is being disruptive to the learning of others.
* Staff – if you have the luxury of additional staff in your classroom, then direct them beforehand to speak quietly to the child about their behaviour.
* If you don't have that luxury, and if this is a recurring difficulty, *speak to the child before and after the lesson*, to discuss the impact that their choice in behaviour is having on others. Agree on a sign that you will make to communicate to them that they are doing this. This should help reduce the shouting out.

71

We all know that I could quite easily write several chapters on low-level disruption and continually add to the topic. The difficulties continue to come year on year, but, rest assured, by reading these entries, your behaviour toolkit will continue to grow, and you will feel empowered and able to deal with inappropriate behaviour effectively.

There are some good ideas and advice on how to use plenaries online at: www.teachertoolkit.co.uk/2017/05/22/plenaries

Must follow on Twitter:

@behaviourteach – my account, but seek out the hashtag #behaviourchat. It is a term-time chat from 8.00 to 8.30 pm.

Review of Low-level Behaviour

Date	Strategy	Impact	Children it supported	Amendments

For low-level behaviour, one strategy that works for some children may need to be swapped for another, so it is important to keep track of strategies, as well as to monitor their effectiveness. Use the above table as a tracker. It will also provide supporting evidence if you have to work with any outside agencies on strategies.

MOOD HOOVERS

I love the term 'mood hoover', although I don't love the effect that it has on a classroom and school. 'Mood hoover' means different things to different people. To me, it is the person who drains the positivity from every situation, then zaps the final ounce of positive energy just because they want to. I imagine you are smiling because you are picturing the mood hoover in your workplace. Mood hoovers aren't limited to education. You will know the mood hoover among your neighbours, your friends and even your family. In these settings, we always act differently or have strategies that we use in order to dilute mood hoovers, so why don't we have them in our educational settings? As positive as you are, as much energy as you bring to the classroom, you are only as strong as your weakest member, which translates to the fact that you are as positive as your most negative team member. I can feel the positivity draining from you as I type – but stop! I am going to guide you through strategies to dilute the mood hoovers in your school, and you may even find them turning into the strongest and most positive members of your team. Is your energy coming back? I hope so.

You will find many more mood hoovers when you are discussing behaviour. People don't find behaviour easy and mood hoovers tend to come together on this point. It is far less of an effort being a mood hoover than it is to work hard at behaviour all the time. The way you handle mood hoovers will need different approaches, depending on your position within school.

CLASS TEACHER

If you are a class teacher without any additional support staff in your classroom, then I have the best news – you control the positivity:

> I have come to the frightening conclusion that I am the decisive element. It is my per-
> sonal approach that creates the climate. It is my daily mood that makes the weather . . .
> In all situations, it is my response that decides whether a crisis is escalated or
> de-escalated, and a person is humanised or de-humanised. If we treat people as
> they are, we make them worse. If we treat people as they ought to be, we help them
> become what they are capable of becoming.
>
> Haim G. Ginott (1993[1972])

This quote really does say it all. You set the weather; you decide the atmosphere – positive or negative.

If you are a class teacher with additional support staff, then you actively need to set the level of positivity in your classroom and in your practice, in order to dilute any mood hoovers in your team. I would like to take this opportunity to say that a mood hoover isn't someone having a bad day – we all have those. We all have doubts about whether our approach is correct or even effective – that's normal. Mood hoovers actively moan about your approaches; they don't support you in proactively spotting positive behaviours or providing rewards.

The following are some strategies you can try to counteract mood hoovers:

- At the beginning of each term (at least) sit down with your team to discuss the expectations that you have. Infuse this with positivity and always have your discussions in a positive light.
- Be public with your positive behaviour spotting, for example: 'Mr X, do you see how well John is sitting on his chair?' It automatically brings someone into a positive light.

- Be open and honest when things aren't going right. Sit down to discuss the situation, but have an attitude of 'What next?'. It will avoid the negativity bubbling or even breeding. It portrays that attitude of continual drive to improve, and sets out your high expectations of all staff.

MIDDLE LEADERSHIP/DEPARTMENT LEADS

The more responsibilities that you have in an educational setting, the more widespread your positivity can be. The above strategies are very important, but on a wider team level, as follows:

- At the beginning of your phase or departmental meetings, start with a positive agenda item. Ask your team to share positive news as the first agenda item. The fact that it is first on the agenda shows how important positivity is. The more positivity people hear, the better. Depending on how big your phase or department is, you may want to target specific people to share for the sake of time. This can also be a positive, as it could be a chance to turn mood hoovers into regularly sharing positivity.
- Know your team – if you see that a member of your phase or department is struggling with a mood hoover in their class team, then have a conversation with that person. Ask if they would like your support on building positivity, or if they would like you to have a conversation with the member of staff who is the mood hoover. Sometimes, a member of staff you consider to be negative wouldn't in their wildest dreams describe themselves in that way, and a little conversation could make a huge impact.

CASE STUDY - *Primary*

A primary school implemented a small change to the beginning of staff meetings by asking staff for positives that had happened during that week. At first, it was tricky to get staff to open up and not focus on negatives (whether solution-focused or not), but after a period of time, staff began sharing with enthusiasm. The following year, there were so many things to share that it needed to be focused at each staff meeting – e.g., Early Years Foundation Stage (EYFS) and Year 3, and then Year 1 and Year 4 the week after, etc. This approach also ensured that the mood hoovers on the team shared positivity as well as hearing others' positivity.

SENIOR LEADERSHIP

All the strategies above must be implemented at this level, but we have to be honest that sometimes even when all of them are implemented, there are some mood hoovers who cannot be turned around. However, in your role you are able to influence the delegation of staff. Keep this in mind when you place your staff. Split the mood hoovers so that the negativity cannot bubble, deepen and spread. Once the mood hoovers are diluted, you will have more of a chance to ensure that your school is a positive place of work.

I do hope that I have taken you from a flat feeling to a feeling of empowerment, ready to share your positivity with everyone in your workplace and to convert those mood hoovers who are in your mind right now. Good luck!

Must follow on Twitter:

@abbiemann1982 – a shining beacon of positivity and a great follow for well-being.

REFERENCE

Ginott, H.G. (1993[1972]) *Teacher and Child: A Book for Parents and Teachers*. New York: Scribner.

Staff Shout Out

Complete this activity as part of a staff or departmental meeting. Write a 'post it' to share with another colleague. It will ensure that someone feels good about themselves.

aNIMAL THERAPY

A strong lesson that I learnt early on in my career involved animals. I wasn't even thinking about supporting children with their behaviour when I wanted to be able to have animals in our school. I wanted to support children in understanding about having responsibility for an animal, their environment, and also to have the chance to learn about earning money (from produce) and to buy necessities (animal feed and essentials). Although the thought of linking animals with supporting children with their behaviour hadn't entered my mind at this point, I did have an active interest in child psychology and supporting children with their behaviour. At the point of this project, I did have a few children whose behaviour was difficult.

CASE STUDY - Zebulon - Primary School

I remember the day it clicked for me. I was cleaning out the animals and one of my children, Zebulon, who was struggling with his behaviour at lunchtimes, had come to find me. He wanted to cool off and talk through how he was feeling. He always struggled to communicate his difficulties, so the beginning part of the interaction involved him being non-verbal, while I continued cleaning out the animals and he calmed down. After a while, he asked if he could help me with the cleaning out, and as we were working, he opened up communications about the issues that he was having that lunchtime. I was able to support him through conflict resolution. This wasn't the end. The next morning, he was by the animals when I went to feed them. He wanted to feed them with me. He became a regular fixture in looking after the animals. He was kind, compassionate, responsible – three words that others might not have used to describe him. The animals enabled him to show his strengths in a different way. It gave him a purpose to come to school on time, and to choose the correct behaviours (when he could), as some of his behaviours were as a result of a diagnosis that he received during his time at our school. It is an outcome like this that urges me to talk to other teachers to implement something similar in *every* school in case it unlocks the potential in one child. For one child alone, it is worth it. The icing on the cake was that, by the time Zebulon finished at our school, the animals loved him more than they loved me.

If any senior leadership team need to be persuaded to have animals in your school, then tell them that story. If they need persuading even further, then give them other facts and show them the benefits of having an animal or animals (if you're lucky) in the school grounds:

- Animals are a great context to help learning. They can easily be added into word problems and incorporated into schemes of work.
- Animals enrich your school experience. If you know anyone who has had the privilege of having a pet at school, they value that experience and it's what makes them smile when they think of their school memories.
- Animals will improve school attendance – children will want to come to school to spend time with the animals, just as Zebulon did in my case study.
- Emotional well-being – many children will choose the option of spending time with their pet when they are feeling upset.
- Homework – many children prefer to do their homework when their pet is in the vicinity.
- Animals encourage nurturing – children soon learn that to gain an animal's trust and love, they need to be kind and gentle with them, which builds their nurturing skills.
- Animals create a sense of responsibility in children.
- Animals become very good friends to children. Some children struggle to have any friends, so guaranteeing them one during their time at school is important.
- Improvement in attainment – you may have heard about 'reading dogs', which works on the principle that children (particularly those who are reluctant readers) read to a dog.

Similarly, while some children prefer to do their homework with a dog close to them, others prefer to read to their pet. It is likely to increase your children's desire to read, improve their attendance and, in turn, increase their reading ability.

HOW TO COPE IF AND WHEN YOUR SCHOOL ANIMAL DIES

This is a rather morbid subheading, but we have to be factual and realistic about the life spans of animals. Unfortunately, we do need to prepare our children for the eventuality that a pet animal may die and how to cope with it effectively if and when it happens. It's such a stressful and emotional time when a school animal dies. In order to prepare a child for any loss in their life, we need to build characteristics in them like resilience and awareness. There are some strategies that you can use to support children during this difficult time:

- Be sensitive to the fact that this may be the first time your children have experienced loss. They may have an understanding of death through conversations, books, the media, etc., but if this is their first experience of death, it needs to be dealt with sensitively. To avoid confusion, be clear and concise with your language. Explain that unfortunately the school animal has died. You don't need to explain any further, just wait for their questions and go from there.

- You can build on the fact that this is not an individual loss. Your whole school has lost a creature close to them, so children can find comfort by discussing this with each other. You can discuss this further during PSHE (Personal, Social, Health and Economic) education, citizenship or tutor sessions. This may encourage children to be reflective about their loss.

As a member of school staff, you can support your children through whatever is shared during these reflections. If there are children whose behaviour makes you feel that you need to seek external advice on how best to cope with any behaviours being presented during this loss, you could start with parents and go from there.

Must follow on Twitter:

@cherrylkd and her dog Doodles; join their adventures in a school.

Rainbow Bridge

When you work with a child around the loss of an animal, you may want to discuss with them (depending on their age) that they can remember their pet in a happy way and that it is simply on a rainbow bridge. Use this resource to draw their pet on a rainbow bridge. Ask the child to colour in the rainbow bridge.

OUTDOOR LEARNING

When we talk about learning, the majority of people assume that learning takes place in a classroom. When we discuss strategies for managing behaviour or inspiring learning, then we imagine this taking place in a classroom. Learning can, of course, take place outdoors, and there are so many lessons that children can learn from nature. When we really focus on thinking about outdoor learning, the assumptions are that we may be discussing PE, geography or children in pre-school or early years education. We're not. We're going to look at how children's behaviour can be supported by lessons in the outdoors and where you can facilitate further learning.

FARM SCHOOLS

A farm school is exactly as it sounds. It is a regular school setting, with an on-site working farm, where the children are responsible for the running of the farm, day-to-day general operations, any selling of produce, budgetary responsibilities and responsibility for their upkeep, along with lessons that derive from any of these.

CASE STUDY - Secondary

Flag Farm School is a secondary school. They have the following motto and vision when providing education for their secondary students: they want their children to leave Flag Farm School with the qualifications and skills that will equip them for later life. However, sitting alongside that, the leadership team at Flag Farm School want to ensure that the children leave with the life skills that they learn from being in such a setting. The variety of intellectual, emotional and social skills that they can gain from learning in a farm setting is astounding and, most certainly, invaluable.

There are several features to the curriculum at Flag Farm School which make it unique and distinctive, and ensure that children get a very different curriculum:

- The school offers higher project-based learning. Up to 30 per cent of its timetable is offered as project learning. Project-based learning is designed to get children to work for an extended period of time, embarking on investigations, responding to complex questions, working with problems and/or being appropriately challenged. These projects are designed to take place during the outdoor learning on the farm.
- Children are all in mixed-age classes when they complete their work around the farm. The work undertaken at the school is described as not following age ranges, but allowing children to work at the actual level they are. Flag Farm School matches its curriculum to the needs of the children. The school is aware of the strengths, difficulties and needs of each of its children, and creates courses to enable them to fulfil their individual potential.
- Flag Farm School works as a democracy. There is a weekly student parliament, where decisions are made with the children. Their opinions are respected and theirs is a genuine voice in decision-making.
- Flag Farm School is strong on relationship building. They offer one-to-one counselling support for children who need additional social, emotional and mental health support. They also offer one-to-one additional tutoring for those who have English as an additional language and those with special educational needs.

As a result of this pupil involvement and individually tailored curriculum, behavioural incidents are extremely low. However, if and when they do arise, they are dealt with using conflict resolution and restorative justice.

I can appreciate that Flag Farm School can be perceived as the 'gold standard' of outdoor provision, but there is nothing stopping you from providing the basic principles of outdoor learning for your children. There are a few things that you can implement straight away, getting as involved as you would like to:

- Learning outside – the key to this is not simply moving the learning outdoors. It is one of the most common misconceptions that completing the same work outside is outdoor learning. It's certainly one I was guilty of when I first started investigating the principles early on in my career. It needs some careful planning. Think through questions when you are trying to enhance learning through outdoor provision, such as 'What elements of outdoor learning can enhance this learning?', 'How best can I facilitate this learning?', 'Are there any resources that I can ensure are close?', 'Are there any safety principles that I need to address before undertaking the work?'

- Growing fruit and vegetables – some schools may not have the space for an allotment, but, regardless of space, you can still grow basic vegetables. There are vegetables that you can grow very easily, such as radishes in small pots. They take a matter of weeks and children can see the process. Another favourite that we used to do as a class was growing tomatoes and potatoes. Tomatoes can simply grow in a pot, and children can have the experience of being actively involved in keeping the plant alive in order to gain a good crop. Potatoes can be grown in a bucket in the classroom and, again, will need to be looked after. This is an activity that the children really enjoy, as they cannot see the fruits of their labour until the crop is fully grown. If you have room in the outdoor spaces of your school to go one step further and have a raised bed or even a greenhouse, the possibilities are endless.

- Animals – I remember at school having a class rabbit or hamster. The lessons we learned from that around care, responsibility and even loss were something that gave us a good basis from which to experience future challenges. You may like to pursue those lessons in your own classroom, or you may want to look at having animals for the whole school, such as chickens. Children can learn the above lessons, but they can also learn about paying for feed, mucking out, collecting and selling eggs and using the proceeds to pay for the upkeep of the animals. All these elements support a building up of the character traits in children that will enable them to become well rounded and prepared for the next stages in their lives. You can support this further by using these implemented ideas to create personalised curriculums where needed. For the most impact, link this with your pastoral team.

FOREST SCHOOL

There is a wealth of information on Forest Schools as an effective environment for learning. The Forest School Association (www.forestschoolassociation.org/what-is-forest-school) offers more information should you be interested in developing your practice. Forest School is a specialised learning approach that takes place in a woodland or a natural environment with trees. Learners have opportunities to develop confidence and self-esteem through hands-on learning experiences. Its roots originated in the work of early years pioneers in outdoor education and in Scandinavian practice. Put simply, Forest School is a series of regular sessions where children learn skills and knowledge outside. Some schools create their own forest area, using a disused piece of land and growing their own trees for den building and/or shade.

CASE STUDY - Primary

Barge Primary School has 420 children and is considered to be a medium-sized primary school. It is committed to providing learning for children in an outdoor space. The school believes that by taking learning outside, it is providing solid opportunities to build children's self-esteem and well-being, while supporting their behaviour, encouraging their cooperation with others and building their problem-solving skills. All this learning sits alongside academic learning, as it supports children so that they are ready to learn academically. Barge Primary School uses its Personal, Social, Health and Economic (PSHE) education curriculum and plans Forest School opportunities to enhance this learning. It runs the Forest School programme, which builds on children's natural instinct to learn and their natural curiosity. They are encouraged to explore different learning opportunities in an outdoor setting. These opportunities allow them to make their own choices when it comes to their learning, as well as the rarer opportunities of taking and managing their own risks. This is something that they tend to experience during typical academic learning. In having these opportunities, Barge Primary School has seen an increase in positive attitudes and positive behaviour.

As with Flag Farm School, the sessions are led by the interests of the learners. The activities covered can incorporate experiences such as building shelters, woodland craftwork, telling stories, cooking over fires, climbing trees, hunting for mini-beasts and making habitats for them, and the very popular activity of making mud pies. Woodland tools are introduced as the programme develops. This extends learning and provides new opportunities for risk management. As well as an increase in positive learning attitudes and positive behaviour, Barge Primary School found that by taking the majority of their learning outdoors, regardless of weather, the children began to show a change in character – e.g., they became more resilient, confident and independent learners.

I'm sure that this chapter has got your mind buzzing with ways in which you can implement outdoor learning in your curriculum offering. The following books and Twitter feed will help you to get started:

Children Learning Outside the Classroom by Sue Waite (https://uk.sagepub.com/en-gb/eur/children-learning-outside-the-classroom/book244871) or *Forest School in Practice* by Sara Knight (https://uk.sagepub.com/en-gb/eur/forest-school-in-practice/book249142) for additional ideas and lesson plans, and for more information on how to set up this kind of provision.

Must follow on Twitter:

@**LittlForestFolk** – an outstanding forest school nursery catering for children at 2–5 years old. It is full of practical ideas that you can implement at any age.

Journey Sticks

This is an activity that you can complete outdoors with relative ease and minimal planning, and that will create lots of fun and discussion.

All you need is one small stick per child (or go on your adventure knowing that you'll be able to find a stick when you arrive), a variety of coloured string, scissors and crayons. Everything else you can find on your journey, which is the beauty of this activity.

As your journey begins (and after you've found the perfect stick for each child), choose a colour of string and wrap it around your stick to signify the beginning of your journey.

Hunt for different items on your adventure and tie them to your stick. They will serve as a reminder of your journey. Continue this until the end of your adventure.

When you get home and for time to come, you will be able to retell your adventure by looking at your journey stick and you'll have a representation of the fun that you had.

Adaptations can be made in different ways, as follows:

- Tie your stick to a piece of cardboard for younger children so that they can be supported with completing it themselves.
- Older children can carve their journey sticks on to blocks of wood.

PARENTS

Parents are invaluable stakeholders. We always focus on children, as we should, but we can make much more of a difference and impact if we have the support of a child's parent or carer/adult at home. Developing good relationships with parents and carers is the best way forward to support children with behaviour, and they can be pivotal in realising a change in a child's behaviour. However, just as with anyone, parents have a variety of different personalities and these need managing in different situations. We usually learn about how to work with parents by our experiences 'on the job', but this chapter will give you a head start.

BASIC ADVICE FOR DEALING WITH PARENTS

There are pieces of advice that may seem basic, but I guarantee there will be ideas that you will have overlooked, so read the following and reflect over things that you may have forgotten:

- Remember that the child you are discussing with the parent is their child. This may seem obvious, but I know many people get caught up in the message that they are trying to convey without remembering the very important fact that the message you are giving is about somebody's baby – be sensitive.
- Understand that the right time for you may not be the right time for them. If you want to talk to a parent, then explain that you want to have a short conversation and ask when the best time is for them. It means that both of you will have the time to dedicate to the conversation. Rushed conversations can become heated very quickly.
- Understand that your preferred method of communication may not be theirs. Also remember that you may need to use several methods of communication with parents in your class. Some parents like to talk face-to-face. Some parents may want to have the conversation on the telephone and some may prefer to communicate by email.
- Know their child – again, I appreciate this seems very obvious, but you would be surprised how often people have been confused about who they are talking about. Imagine how this must feel to a parent – straight away there is a loss of trust or belief in you as a teacher and a protector of their child.

Once you have read through these strategies, reflect on situations where these may not have been at the forefront of your mind when preparing to talk to parents.

PARENTS' EVENING

The above ideas for support roll into the following strategies, which will then roll into following sections:

- Make sure that you are well prepared for your parents' evening. Although it seems like a short session, you have to cover so much in that time, so unless you are well prepared, it will be wasted time or even uncomfortable time.
- Being prepared means being clear on what you want to discuss. You should speak with clarity and what you say should be well thought out. The best piece of advice that I can share with you is to start by asking parents if they have any questions. It will help you to stick to your timings. The worst thing is if you talk for the whole time slot and then the parents have further questions. You will feel that you can't cut off a parent if they have genuine questions, but you will then overrun, which will have a negative knock-on effect on your other appointments.

- Always be honest. Look below at how to deliver difficult messages, but do not brush them aside. It may well make things easier for you, but it does an actual disservice to the child and you are really making things more difficult for your colleagues who will, at some point, have to communicate that message, which will be even harder if you haven't started discussions earlier in the child's school experience.

DIFFICULT CONVERSATIONS WITH PARENTS

There will always be those messages that we will find difficult to communicate and those that we are unsure how to communicate. Preparation is key to delivering these difficult messages successfully.

- Write down the points you want to talk about on a notepad. Stick to these in your conversations. Waffle won't help you; it won't calm down any emotion and it will certainly take away the clarity from your message. You will end up not delivering your message correctly and you will have to have a repeat conversation.

- Use the previous strategies of arranging an appropriate time and preferred method of communication for your meeting. Whenever and wherever the meeting takes place, make sure that it is private. If you are having a discussion around behaviour, then you know that emotions can overtake a situation and it could be embarrassing to the parent if others are around. Just to note, it isn't an embarrassing situation, but we must be mindful that it *may* cause embarrassment.

- My aim isn't to put off any teacher from having a difficult conversation, but if you are having a face-to-face meeting, then be careful about where your meeting takes place. Early on in my teaching career I had my last parents' evening appointment in my classroom in a mobile away from the main building. It wasn't a meeting that I was expecting to be at all difficult, so I hadn't thought through any strategies for managing a difficult conversation as there were no difficult messages to convey. However, the parent became aggressive and I was quickly intimidated. I was situated away from the door, it was dark and all the other teachers had finished and left. My advice is to either arrange all the appointments in a communal area or ensure that you are near a door and are not alone in a building. Just for the record, I got up and left.

Must follow on Twitter:

@ParentHub_UK – this organisation provides free support on parental engagement in schools.

Difficult Conversations

As discussed in this entry, it is very important to focus on your thoughts before having a difficult conversation, so use the space below to note down your thoughts:

1. _____

2. _____

3. _____

4. _____

5. _____

Key Points From The Conversation

_____

_____

_____

_____

Actions To Move Forward

_____

_____

_____

_____

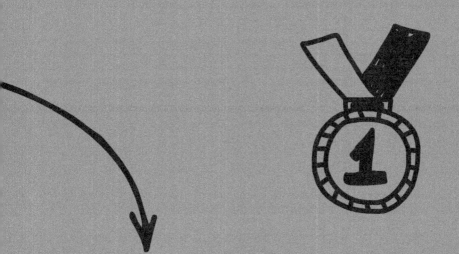

QUALITY
FIRST
TEACHING

Quality is one of the foundations that supports you with behaviour in your classroom. If your teaching isn't well prepared, executed on an individual basis or well thought through, there is the opportunity for behaviour issues to arise.

If you think about when you've had an unexpected change to your day or something hasn't gone to plan, you feel flustered. This is totally normal and will happen in day-to-day life in a school. However, it allows for unstructured time. Chatting will start, children start to fiddle with equipment, chatting gets louder, disruption increases and it's at that point that negative behaviour can really escalate. Now, no one is expecting you to be able to have your day planned to in an inch of its life and be able to avoid all these situations. That really wouldn't be possible – if it was, then let me know how, but you can have some activities on the back burner that will enable you to cope in these situations.

PRIMARY

- Have some reasoning challenges ready for children to work through. It will promote conversation and direct discussion in a positive way rather than having it spill over in a negative way.

- Quick-fire questions – throw out some times tables questions or general questions linked to your learning to keep the children learning during these periods of free time. This suggestion does come with a caveat, though. Even though they are quick-fire questions, you must give your children some processing time before moving on or helping them. If you do not give this thinking time in situations that are time pressured, you may cause a certain level of frustration, which may even cause disruption.

- Newsround – CBBC uploads a daily news bulletin on its website. It is engaging for all ages of children. It is approximately 10 minutes long, and you can ask questions afterwards. It promotes positive discussion, enables children to understand about events happening in their own country and gives them a chance to understand the world in which they live.

CASE STUDY – Primary – Amir – Year 5

Amir is a 9-year-old boy in Year 5. He exhibits low-level behaviour difficulties and often disrupts the learning of others during transition times. During a discussion as a staff team, it was highlighted that these transition times are a consistent weak spot and that if Amir is given an alternative task, then the low-level behaviour reduces. As a staff team, it was decided to create the challenges, reasoning tasks and discussion questions that Amir could use during these transition times to keep him focused. It had immediate impact and reduced the transition times as a potential hotspot.

SECONDARY

- The quick-fire questions are also applicable to secondary students. You can make these subject specific and ensure that learning continues at all opportunities.

- Self-study – if free time is going to be 5 minutes or more, then direct your children to complete some self-study on the topic they are covering. It will support them in over-learning and will enable low-level behaviour to be kept to a minimum.

- Project-based learning – children can have a project book around their current learning that they can pick up and work with. This can be a blank scrapbook or one of the exercise books that would stay in your resource room for years if not used. It is an opportunity for children to be creative, whether it is topic-related artwork, designs for a new product, etc. It can all be dependent on the topic that it is focused on. It can be focused for groups or for individuals, depending on the needs of your class. It's not something that will need any marking, as you can verbally discuss any progress or support.

PLANNING PROCESS

The planning process is very important when supporting behaviour. When you are thinking through the planning of your lessons, have the children in mind who struggle with behaviour. Think about the start of your lesson. How will they react? How will they learn best? Then think about transitions from input to individual learning. Do they need to transition first? Or last? What is most appropriate for them?

Can the children work on an individual basis or will they need a scaffold? Is it a child who needs timed check-ins from you to ensure that they are on track with their learning? By check-in, I mean just wandering by to have a look and give a visual clue if they are working well. It will reassure a child that they should continue in the same vein. Obviously, if they are struggling or off-task, then you can use some of the strategies detailed in the entry on low-level disruption to get them back into focus.

Will any part of the lesson involve group work? Is this an aspect that they will struggle with? Is there a particular set of pupils who will work well with the child in your mind and enable them to fulfil their potential and learn in the most effective way? Or does the child struggle so much that they just need to complete the activity individually? There is no point in forcing children to learn in a social situation if it is something that they find extremely difficult. Use your focused interventions to support them to build this capacity and improve in this area, and then introduce it into your lessons that way.

Where is the child sitting? Can children sit where they want in your lesson? Is this appropriate with your child? If not, again, support your child to make the right choice. Use diversion to get your child to sit in an effective place – e.g., 'Jamie, can you sit here today? I need you to help me with something?' – or sit them with a particular child so that the seating arrangements take care of themselves.

REFLECTION

Due to time pressures in the school environment, the reflective parts of lessons are more often than not condensed or even missed. This can mean that the same mistakes are made over and over again, and behaviour escalates and becomes repetitive or even a habit. The more times you plan a lesson with the children in mind, the better you will become at understanding the best way to teach the individual needs of your children. As well as providing periods of reflection in your lessons (which we know is very important), find periods to reflect in your planning and delivery.

Must follow on Twitter:

@tes – TES provides free resources in teaching for you to pop straight into your lesson plans.

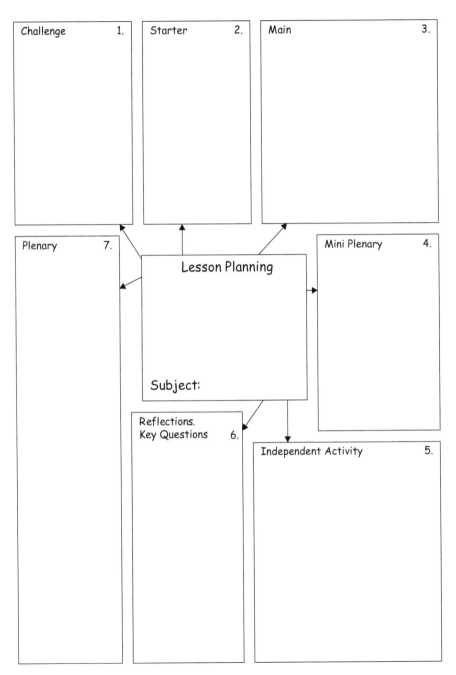

| Challenge 1. | Starter 2. | Main 3. |

Plenary 7.

Lesson Planning

Subject:

Mini Plenary 4.

Reflections.
Key Questions 6.

Independent Activity 5.

RELATIONSHIPS

It is quite a big statement for me to make, but if you don't have relationships with your children, you won't have anything. This doesn't just apply to learning but also to behaviour. Relationships are the magic wand that you have been searching for. Now for the disappointment: they will not eliminate difficult behaviours. However, they will support you in being able to work with the children in the best possible way. Relationships of the strength that you need aren't easy to develop. They involve a child being able to trust that you will do what you say, that you will keep them safe and have their best interests at heart. To create those relationships, do what you say, follow through with the actions that reflect what you say, do everything in your power to keep the children safe, show them that you are keeping them safe, discuss your reasons for certain decisions and explain that you have their best interests at heart. For some children, this will be the first time that they have encountered somebody willing to do such a thing for them.

CASE STUDY – Primary – Nathan

Nathan is a 7-year-old boy in a Year 3 class. He is a lively character with a real charm. Nathan's teacher has a good relationship with him and he works hard in the class, tries his best and enjoys positive relationships with his peers. Nathan has two younger siblings. When he is at school, he constantly talks about them, how they are developing and growing, what they like to play with and who their friends are. He appears to really worry about how his siblings are getting on in school and will look out for them at breaktimes and lunchtimes. There have even been times when Nathan has asked his teachers questions about his siblings' homework and explained that he helps them with it.

Nathan's behaviour can be quite tricky in terms of the fact that he can be unpredictable in his reactions. He can be frustrated when he doesn't get the answer that he wants to hear from an adult and he will do what he wants to do anyway, despite warnings of the consequences. He cannot understand the reasons for his teachers' decisions when they are explained to him. Discussions continued with Nathan throughout his year and it unfolded that the reason Nathan couldn't understand his teachers' decisions or their answers he didn't want to accept was because at home he made the decisions himself. He was a mini adult in effect: he supported his siblings and he looked after himself. He didn't have to rely on waiting for decisions from others, so he was not used to listening to adults and having to do as they asked. He could not understand why decisions were made for him and why he had to abide by someone else's decision on what was best. It took a while for Nathan to really develop a relationship with his teachers as, even though he 'got on well' with people, he didn't believe that they had his best interests at heart. He didn't see why they should, as he could look after himself. His teacher had to frame the interventions around the fact that the teacher was an adult and he was a child. This wasn't meant to make Nathan feel like a 'baby', but it was a fact, and the usual way of things is for adults to look after children.

CASE STUDY – Secondary – Fatima – Year 8

Fatima has a similar background to Nathan. She took on the majority of care for her younger siblings and, of course, herself. She is often one of the last through the door in the morning and is always in a rush. Her appearance is often unkempt. She is very distrusting of adults, will use abusive language and will not engage in conversations with them. She has a small circle of friends with whom she seems to enjoy positive relationships, but she struggles with other groups of friends. She could be considered a target for other friendship groups due to her appearance and volatile behaviour. Other children wind her up, watch her get upset, then enjoy the fall-out.

Mrs Johnson stands on the gate every morning to greet the children. Her role is also to challenge any disruptive behaviour from the children coming into school as well as check whether their uniform is being worn incorrectly. Every morning she greets Fatima but does not get a response or even an acknowledgement. The well-being team have Fatima on their radar and are trying to engage her through group work with her social circle. Although there wasn't an instant improvement in Fatima's demeanour, there was an improvement in the attitude of the group as a whole. Fatima continued to ignore Mrs Johnson on the gate, but other members of the group began to greet her.

During one session and along with other members of the group, Fatima wrote that what made her feel safe in school was that Mrs Johnson greeted her on a daily basis. This was the first time that Fatima had acknowledged the presence of an adult in her school life. After continued work in the group, Fatima began to acknowledge Mrs Johnson along with her friends. This might seem like an incredibly small piece of progress, but to Fatima it was a huge step forward.

To reflect on relationships in school life, think about a member of school staff you recall when you were at school. It doesn't matter if it is primary or secondary. It could be one in each. Why do you remember them? What did they do to make you feel that they knew you? The fact that you still remember them is down to relationships. Now try to repeat those relationships with the children in your school.

Must follow on Twitter:

@chrischivers2 – Chris Chivers' knowledge on the development of relationships is most definitely worth following.

Behaviour Jenga

Tell me a good manner. Win 2 pts	Someone in your class calls you a rude name. Tell me two things that you could do. Win 4 pts
Your teacher has big ears. What could you call him? Win 2 pts	You chose the wrong behaviour going into the hall. Minus 5 pts
A child is running too fast in the playground and bumps into you. Tell me one thing that you could do. Win 2 pts	You're in assembly and it's really boring. Tell me one thing that you could do. Win 2 pts
You've got a warning. Minus 2 pts	You've had no warnings for two weeks. Win 10 pts
Show me your best smile. Win 2 pts	You are swinging on your chair and you accidentally rock on to someone's toe. What can you do to make it better? Win 4 pts
Your teacher has food on their jumper. What could you say to them? Win 2 pts	Someone has really upset you. Tell me two ways that you can calm yourself down. Win 5 pts
It is your worst lesson next. How do you walk into the lesson? Win 2 pts	You threw a pencil. Minus 2 pts
You've earnt a sticker for holding a door for an adult. Win 2 pts	A child you don't know is crying. Tell me two things that you could do. Win 4 pts
Tell me one of the best things that you have ever done. Win 2 pts	You've lost one of your shoes. Tell me two things you could do. Win 4 pts
Someone in your class says something that isn't the right answer. What could you do? Win 2 pts	You see somebody hit your best friend. Tell me two things that you could do. Win 5 pts
Your teacher won't let you answer a question. What could you do? Win 2 pts	You hid someone's things. Minus 2 pts
You shared your crisps at lunch. Win 2 pts	A child in Reception is crying because they can't read. How could you help them? Win 4 pts

Tell me the best day you've had at school. Win 2 pts	Tell me how you are feeling today. Win 4 pts
Someone blames you for breaking a lunchbox and you know it wasn't you. What should you do? Win 2 pts	You lied. How could you correct it? Win 5 pts
You think something isn't fair. How can you challenge it? Win 2 pts	You interrupted a teacher. Minus 2 pts
You played nicely all lunchtime. Win 2 pts	Someone is sitting on their own at lunch. Tell me three things that you could do. Win 4 pts
What's your favourite game to play with someone else? Win 2 pts	Tell me how you think I'm feeling today. Win 4 pts
You are writing in your book and someone knocks you. What should you do? Win 2 pts	You became angry and hit somebody. What do you do? Win 5 pts
Tell me three things that you should never do at school. Win 2 pts	You said unkind things to someone. Minus 2 pts
You came in smiling today. Win 2 pts	You don't have any food for breaktime. What could you do? Win 4 pts
What is your favourite subject and why? Win 2 pts	Tell me how you know you've had a good day. Win 4 pts
You were sent out. Minus 4 pts	
Tell me three things you could do to earn a certificate. Win 2 pts	
You were friendly in PE. Win 2 pts	

SENIOR LEADERSHIP TEAM

The reason that there is a whole entry on the senior leadership team (SLT) is because they can really make or break behaviour support. An unsupportive SLT can make you feel inadequate as a teacher, and this can be very damaging to a school, to the behaviour of the children and to the self-esteem of the teaching staff. There is no need to discuss any more of the negative things that having a poor SLT can do. I am extremely lucky to have had a supportive SLT, but I appreciate that I have been lucky, so we will focus on how to ensure that you are a supportive senior leadership team.

HOW TO BE A SUPPORTIVE SENIOR LEADERSHIP TEAM

- Read this book. It is all in the attitude of a person. If you are a proactive senior leader and want to do the best for your staff and, in turn, for your children, then you are set to be exceptional. Keep reading, keep learning and keep improvement at the forefront of your mind: personal and school improvement.

- Revisit your behaviour policy (and other policies) regularly. They are a working document, should be reflected on and reviewed on a termly basis (at least). This should involve all the staff who use these documents. On a yearly basis, gain views from all stakeholders on this policy, including children and parents. Ask what is working and what is not.

- Linking to the above, listen and keep on listening. Improvement is also about listening and tweaking. Pupil voice is paramount in this. The behaviour policy directly affects our children, so it would be ridiculous not to include our children in reflections and improvements.

- Model good behaviour and attitudes that you would expect. You are the adult and you make the weather, so continually model the positivity that you want to see in the atmosphere of the school.

- Lead by example. Model talking about behaviour in your school setting. If you do not make behaviour a daily conversation, then you are risking school staff feeling worried about talking about behaviour or asking for help. It is a very thin line between teachers asking for help and/or discussing behaviour, and feeling that people will judge them as being unable to handle behaviour.

- Ban phrases such as 'they behaved for me' and 'I just don't know why they are doing that for you'. When school staff come and speak to you about behaviour, please listen. If they ask for strategies, then provide them or signpost them to further support. If they don't ask, then just listen.

- Introduce termly one-to-one well-being meetings for all members of your teaching staff. Use your senior leadership team, phase leaders and department leaders to complete them, but alternate so you aim to have spoken to every member of the staff by the end of the year. Ideally, complete this with all members of your school staff, but where a school has hundreds of members of school staff, this may not be possible. Among the questions in the one-to-one meetings, ask your staff if they feel supported in dealing with behaviour. They will be honest with you.

CASE STUDY - *Secondary*

The senior leadership team faced unrest among a few members of staff, and although the majority of the staff seemed happy in their jobs, there was a feeling of unhappiness and 'corridor gossip'. As a result, the SLT implemented the one-to-one well-being meetings (see the photocopiable resource at the end of the section). They decided who would interview which member of staff, based on which staff would open up the most. Once they received feedback, they were able to act on it in order to improve the atmosphere for everyone.

HOW TO PRESENT YOUR IDEAS TO THE SENIOR LEADERSHIP TEAM

If you are a member of the school staff, I know you will have an abundance of ideas that are integral for both school improvement and moving forwards. It is important to have an understanding of the wider picture. Just as I've said for the senior leadership team to lead by example and support all members of their school staff, it is important for other school staff to try to see the bigger picture that the SLT thinks about. By thinking in this way, you can consider how to present your idea in the best way.

- If you need to approach the senior leadership team with a problem, try to think of a solution that you can present at exactly the same time. There is a limit on time within a school day, and rather than presenting the SLT with a problem and the team having to go away and think of a solution, the problem could be discussed and resolved straight away.

- If you want to discuss an idea that you would like to implement or share further, think about the wider picture of what your idea would mean for the school. First, think through the positives that would come as a result of implementing your idea. Have you managed to trial this approach in your own department or class? Is there an impact that you can discuss? You need to communicate these positives and the impact they could have within school. Think through the possible barriers to implementing your ideas and the potential difficulties that may arise if they are implemented. If you have weighed up these things before you present to the SLT, you will have had time to think through some solutions to suggest. The clearer you are in presenting your idea, the more likely it is that the SLT will accept it, and that it will be implemented and/or supported by them.

A general reflection of this chapter would be to understand each and every person's job role within school. If there is a mutual respect for each other within schools, it will have a positive impact on the teamwork within the school. Again, practising effective teamwork with colleagues will model this to the children within your setting.

Must follow on Twitter:

@sltchat – SLTChat operates a free weekly CPD chat under #sltchat, discussing all things related to senior leadership.

Teacher Well-being One-to-One Meeting	
1.	Do you feel supported in implementing the behaviour policy? Are there any children in your class you have difficulty managing?
Response	
2.	Do you feel that the planning process is supportive?
Response	
3.	Do you feel that the marking and feedback policy supports you in your job?
Response	
4.	Do you find planning in your planning, preparation and assessment (PPA) teams supports you effectively?
Response	
5.	Do you feel that the school invests in your continuing professional development (CPD)? Have you attended any of the collaboratives or training events? How useful is CPD in staff meetings? Is there anything else you would like for the future?
Response	
6.	Do you require further support to enjoy a work–life balance and be an effective teacher?
Response	
7.	Is your competence in assessment growing? Where do you need support?
Response	
8.	Do the moderation opportunities support your teacher judgements?
Response	
9.	Do you feel comfortable approaching any member of the SLT with any concerns you may have? Do you welcome opportunities like this to discuss your role and well-being outside performance management?
Response	
10.	Is there anything you would like to raise as part of this well-being discussion?
Response	

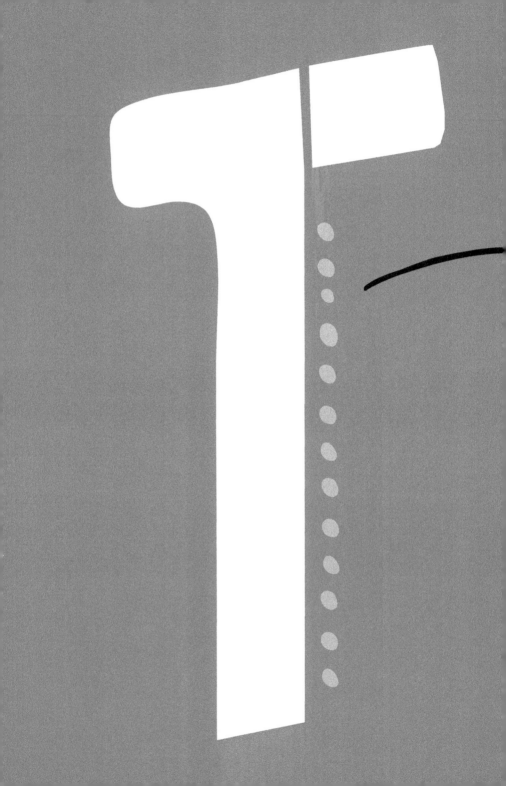

TEACHING ASSISTANTS

Whenever we talk about additional staff in schools, we are greeted with chortles, eye rolling or my personal favourite response of 'as if!'. Additional staff are becoming rarer within a classroom, and many more schools are being reduced to additional adults for one-to-one children only, or are having to reduce them totally to ensure that well-being teams are in place as well as Family Support Workers. This shouldn't be the cause of negativity about budget in schools, but more of a prompt to think clearly about what staff you have and how they can make the most impact on the outcomes of our children.

STAFF SHARING

The best way of sharing expertise within a school in order to enable children to have equal access to additional support or boosters is to create intervention staff teams.

CASE STUDY - Primary - Hall Cross Primary School

Hall Cross Primary School reviewed their school support staffing at the end of term for effectiveness. They faced the dilemma of wanting to ensure school improvement, but needing to invest in behaviour support and well-being teams, as well as providing support for attendance and families. In order to ensure that children were ready to learn, the school realised that they needed to invest in these areas. By moving current support staff into positions within a well-being team – the role of an emotional literacy support assistant and an attendance officer/family support worker – the learning support assistants' team was automatically reduced. This moved away from the previous model of having one learning support assistant per classroom, which had been the model for many years. Teachers were set on the idea that this was the way of getting effective impact and felt that they would struggle without this support.

The head teacher, together with the SLT, worked to improve the confidence of the teachers around this change, and put in place some continuing professional development as a way of doing this. He then mapped out which members of staff he wanted to fulfil the additional roles and discussed it with them. Once he had the expressions of interest confirmed with these members of staff, he went back to his SLT to confirm these places. After this was done, they began to map out the rest of the learning support assistants. He mapped one learning support assistant to each class in pre-school, Early Years Foundation Stage and Key Stage 1 classes. They then split the rest of the learning support assistants between the upper and lower juniors. There were three in the Year 3/4 team and three in the Year 5/6 team. This wasn't the end as the school could not guarantee impact on the progress and outcome of children. As it stood, it looked as if Hall Cross Primary School was losing staff. In conjunction with all these plans, the teachers worked in their phases to complete intervention maps based on previous assessments. This enabled the teachers to see which children had the most needs that required meeting outside quality first teaching. The intervention teams were then focused on these children. Interventions were completed using entry and exit criteria, as well as success criteria. They were measurable: both learning support assistants and teachers could identify straight away where impact was being made, and were able to measure progress as well as target future interventions. These intervention maps could clearly show provision for vulnerable groups, those children that had areas of difficulty, as well as those children who needed boosting or challenging. Another positive impact was that the intervention teams were directed exactly to where they needed to be – there was no wasted time and days were focused on impact, impact and more impact.

HOW TO MAKE YOUR TEACHING ASSISTANT FEEL VALUED

We all know how emotive behaviour can be. A week can be like a rollercoaster. Days can go up and down. You can even have peaks and troughs within hours. This much change within a period of time can cause extremes of feelings. It is important that school staff support each other not only to ensure positivity, but also to support well-being. A member of school staff will put a huge effort into their work – they wouldn't work with children and in school settings if they didn't have the drive and commitment for it. However, we can support them to sustain these efforts by making them feel valued in the following ways:

- If you are a senior leader, then you could ensure that your teaching assistants feel valued by having flexibility. Don't let your school staff miss important events, such as their child's first day at school, their child's nativity, their 25th wedding anniversary, etc. By knowing that you are supporting this member of staff's personal events, you will ensure that they feel valued, but you will also be deepening those relationships that we have talked about in previous entries.

- Invest in the continuing professional development (CPD) of your school staff. Use your performance management system to find out the career aspirations of your support team. By doing this, you can support them by providing opportunities to further their career or explore areas they find particularly interesting. Again, this doesn't need to have huge financial impact. You can use specialists from within your own school to support others and/or observe other practice.

Teaching assistants and other members of school staff are an invaluable resource within your school. Reflect on what has been discussed in this entry and think about how best you can use the suggestions to have the best impact on the outcomes of your children.

For further ideas on how you can support well-being within your school staff, please have a look at the 'Well-being' entry. You may also like to dip into the 'Yellow' entry to look at ideas on how to promote positive mental health.

Must follow on Twitter:

@emwot1 – EmmaWot1 is an incredible member of support staff who constantly shares ideas on how to support children with behaviour difficulties.

Use this tracker for communication. It will allow your teaching assistant to write down their ideas, and for you to have the opportunity to value them and discuss them with your colleagues.

General Intervention Monitoring

Name of Intervention:

LSA/TA/Teacher Name: **Year Group**

USE RAG

Date	Objective	Pupil/s Present	Comments/Notes

UNMET NEEDS

The behaviour difficulties that you can see in a classroom may be deeper than simply looking at it from one perspective. Behaviour can be a product of an unmet need. We have already explored attachment in our first chapter and how a baby who has unmet needs during the first stage of his or her life can exhibit behaviour difficulties at a later stage. However, it's important to look deeper into special educational needs and how behaviour difficulties can mask these. Unfortunately, there are many children who are excluded from a school setting because it is their behaviour difficulties that have been focused on and reacted to, rather than digging down and exploring other reasons behind the behaviour.

HOW CAN SENDCOS SUPPORT BEHAVIOUR?

Typically, the Special Educational Needs and Disability Coordinator (SENDCo) and behaviour mentor act separately. In best practice they work alongside each other and communicate effectively, as their needs can intertwine. There needs to be a system in place in order to effectively identify concerns, diagnose needs where necessary and act accordingly.

WHAT CAN BE PUT IN PLACE TO EFFECTIVELY SUPPORT CHILDREN?

- An effective system to share concerns – have an initial concerns form. This needs to gather as much evidence as possible and include their date of birth, previous attainment, any prior concern, parental opinion, opinion of other school staff, medical needs, etc. The current teacher who has the concerns needs to fill out this form with as much detail as they can to ensure that it can be directed as efficiently as possible to help the child.

- Teachers need to approach parents or guardians to check when the child's last hearing and eyesight checks were completed. This may seem rather random, but by digging down you can quickly find out if it is a hearing, sight or colour-blindness difficulty. Sometimes it is only at the end of the chain of investigations that the child's needs are met and learning can continue.

- Once this initial concerns form has been submitted and if there isn't a positive outcome in terms of meeting the child's needs via a hearing or sight check, then a meeting should be scheduled between the SENDCo and the behaviour team. As part of this meeting, all parties need to discuss the form and see if there may be a further difficulty to explore or whether this is a behaviour difficulty that needs additional support.

- If it appears to be an unmet need, then the SENDCo and SEND team can investigate further whether the child should be referred to a speech and language therapist, or whether the family should be supported for a referral to a GP/paediatrician or to an educational psychologist. Before doing this, it is important to ensure that you have full assessments on the child's learning needs. Once these avenues have been explored and executed, then a professional will provide advice ensuring that you can fulfil and appropriately target work to the child's individual needs. By doing this, behaviour difficulty will reduce as it only escalates due to the child's frustration at being unable to learn or communicate, or as a result of any other unmet need the child may have.

- If it appears to be a child's behavioural need, then it can be supported using the strategies described throughout the book.

CASE STUDY – Anouk – Secondary – Year 9

Anouk is a girl in Year 9 whose behaviour escalated upon entering her secondary school. She struggled in primary school and always had to rely on additional support. She would easily be distracted and could be disruptive in terms of talking to others when the teacher was talking, not concentrating and fiddling. However, when she came to the secondary school, her behaviour escalated. Anouk became totally disengaged. She became a work refuser and wouldn't even do the most basic things, including writing the date or learning objective, of which she was more than capable. She began to be aggressive verbally, swearing at the teachers or school staff who placed demands on her. This escalated further to damaging school property and indirectly throwing school furniture. She then became violent towards individuals and began throwing things at school staff. Rather quickly, Anouk became at risk of exclusion. Outside agencies became involved, such as Early Help, the local Pupil Referral Unit, etc. At this point, a multi-agency meeting was held and it was decided to look again at the initial process of cause for concern.

Along with external specialists, the behaviour team and SENDCo repeated the initial process. It was at that point that Anouk's low learning levels were highlighted again. When discussing it further, the team realised that the learning levels had been clouded by the extreme behaviour difficulties. The discussion moved to how her behaviour had escalated from the beginning of secondary and, although it seemed that Anouk's behaviour had always been this extreme, it was a gradual increase. It was decided to pinpoint the learning with the support of advice from the educational psychologist. It was not easy to engage Anouk in learning and, due to her work refusal, it was decided to complete some one-to-one tuition sessions alongside a family member. Anouk was much more amenable to learning with this additional family member present, and the tutor was able to start working on the small learning points from the advice provided by the educational psychologist. Due to the progress (albeit small steps) that Anouk was making, it was decided that the tutor could work in lessons with Anouk and that although this had financial implications, it outweighed the possibility of Anouk being excluded and causing further disruption to the learning of others. Anouk took part in the input of the session and then completed work that was tailored to the learning advice from the educational psychologist. Her presence in the input was important as it was essential not to widen the gap further.

By simply continuing day-to-day focusing on the end result of behaviour that is exhibited, unmet needs can be ignored. This can be incredibly dangerous in not providing the most effective support for a child. Be systematic in your approach and determine what the root cause is of the behaviour, or whether it is behaviour difficulties that you are looking at.

Must follow on Twitter:

@**senexchange** – a SEN hub offering a weekly chat on Wednesdays to discuss everything relating to SEND.

Pupil Passport

	I learn best when:	What I find difficult is: (barriers/ gaps to learning)
Photo	Pupil voice: Teacher voice: Parent voice:	Pupil voice: Teacher voice: Parent voice:
Name: Date of Birth: Yr Grp: Class/Teacher:	I am good at: (strengths) Pupil voice: Teacher voice: Parent voice:	The strategies that are helping me to become more independent are: Pupil voice: Teacher voice: Parent voice:
Date: Oct-Jan/Feb-Apr/May-Sept Review Date: Date placed on SEN Record: SEND Stage: SEND Support/ SEND Support Plan/EHCP Pupil Premium: YES/NO Care Plan in place: YES/NO Area of Need: Reading/Writing/ Spelling/Maths/ Social, Emotional and Mental Health (SEMH)/Speech, Language or Communication Need (SpLCN)		

Children that I work well with are:	The resources/aids that help me most are:	I am particularly motivated to learn by/when:

Other key info: (background/history/medical/internal advice and support/external advice and support)

Attendance =   %

This Pupil Passport is most effective when in partnership with pupils, parents, teachers and SENDCo. Please sign below to indicate that you were involved in the writing process of this.

Pupil's signature ....

Teacher's signature ....

Parent's signature ....

SENCo's signature ....

Target TBAT = To be able to….	How will I work towards this target at school/home?	Progress/Notes/Next Steps (Pupil/parent/teacher/LSA comments)
Target 1		

Smart targets are: specific, measurable, achievable, relevant, time-related

Target TBAT = To be able to….	How will I work towards this target at school/home?	Progress/Notes/Next Steps (Pupil/parent/teacher/LSA comments)
Target 2		

Smart targets are: Specific, measurable, achievable, relevant, time-related

Target TBAT = To be able to….	How will I work towards this target at school/ home?	Progress/Notes/Next Steps (Pupil/parent/teacher/LSA comments)
Target 3		

Smart targets are: Specific, measurable, achievable, relevant, time-related

Discussed with parents/carers: Date:

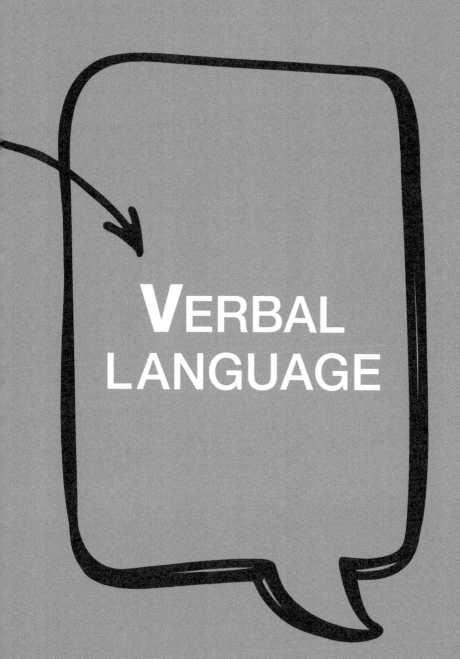

Although we explore primary and secondary settings throughout this book, in this entry we are discussing pre-school. Today, more children are entering pre-school with poor speech and language abilities than ever before. They are growing up at a time when electronic tablets, games consoles and TV are the most popular form of entertainment. Eating at the table and talking with family and friends is rare. Regardless of the reason, we need to change our approach as early as pre-school to make a language-rich environment, and we need to work with families to ensure that this approach is adopted within the family home. You may be wondering why I am talking about speech and language difficulties when this is a book on behaviour. The reason is that behaviour is a form of communication, and by supporting language within your school, you can work to ensure that it does not become an unmet need in any child.

We will look at some language development games from pre-school age, but keep an open mind because pre-school language development games may actually be applicable to some children in secondary school. It isn't something that you go by on age range, but more at a development level.

- Play group games to develop language – put out six pieces of coloured paper and give the children some matching coloured toys/shapes. Get the children to work together to match the coloured toys/shapes to the six pieces of coloured paper. They will reason with each other and use their language skills, including positional language to complete this.

- Play 'I spy' – for those who haven't played it, 'I spy' is a game in which the person 'on' spots something – e.g., a window. They then say 'I spy with my little eye something beginning with w'. The other child/children look around the room for items beginning with 'w' and call out items beginning with 'w' until they get the correct one. The person who gets the answer correct is then on and chooses another item to play with.

- Learn simple and repetitive rhyming songs with actions, such as 'Five Little Speckled Frogs' or 'The Wheels on the Bus'. The finger rhymes and actions support the communication when children complete the rhymes.

- Role play – role-play areas are an excellent way of promoting communication within a group. They also promote the use of imagination. A key prop that allows the development of language within a group setting is a telephone. It gets children talking to whoever they imagine is on the end of the phone, and you'll always find someone to answer it.

- Story sacks – choose a familiar story or fairy tale that the children enjoy. Either provide some props or make some props with the children that you would see in that familiar story or fairy tale. Allow the children to act out their familiar story or fairy tale in a group. This prompts the children to retell the story in their own way. This may be a rather basic retelling, but with the adult support of widening vocabulary and modelling a retell, children will become more elaborate in their retelling over time.

- Story openers – provide the children with story openers and sentence starters. Get the children to form a circle and ask them to use the story openers and sentence starters to create their own story, which supports not only language development but also improves imagination. There's always the support from the teacher who provides the sentence starters and story openers, as well as support from others in the circle.

- Photo prompts – provide the children with a photo prompt. Of course, this can be of anything, but make it engaging. You know what your children are interested in, so tie it into these interests. It's an even easier task if you are working with an individual. By tapping into these interests, the children's language will flow. They won't need to worry about ideas as their prior knowledge will be high. The only rule I suggest is to ban pens. This isn't a writing activity. It is a language activity and the use of a pen will hinder the language element of the activity.

- Farm animals – this is a conversation game. Provide children with two pictures initially of two different animals. Explain that the two animals will be having a conversation and model this for the children. Bear in mind that this can be about absolutely anything. Keep these two animals and ask your child or children to have a conversation between the two animals. Add in another animal to promote further discussion. As you work through this activity over time, you increase the number of animals to promote discussion even further.

- Comic strips – these provide children with a blank comic strip and allow them to create the story itself. The fact that a comic strip uses speech bubbles for its characters means that not only are the children able to practise speech, but also the simple and complex sentences featured in a story.

- International photos – share a photo of something in another country with your child or children along with question prompts: Who? What? When? Where? Why? How? Verbally ask the children to answer these questions in relation to the photo that you presented to them. The question prompts will stimulate language and you can facilitate them to lengthen their answers where necessary.

- What is the same and what is different? Show the children two photographs, which need to be the same in essence but with some differences. Children need to discuss what is similar in the photos and what is different.

- 20 questions – decide what you would like one child to think about. They need to decide on either an object, a sporting team or a celebrity. It really can be your choice, but be consistent. The other person or group then has 20 questions that they can ask to try to determine what the subject is. They are able to guess, but this takes up one of the questions.

In your reflection of this chapter, please choose two games that you will use to promote language in your classroom.

Must follow on Twitter:

@elsasupport – here you can find a wealth of games to play to support all areas of behaviour and emotional well-being.

Inspirational Photo Prompts

WELL-BEING

With all the discussions on behaviour throughout the book, we certainly need to focus on well-being. When you are dealing with behaviour day in and day out, you need to invest in yourself so that you can continue to deal with behaviour every day without it having a detrimental impact on your mental health and well-being. Well-being is not simply for one set of people. It is for everyone – children, staff, stakeholders and *you*. We all need to take an active interest in each other's well-being, because what usually happens is that we are more worried about supporting the well-being of others and neglect our own needs. Thinking of your own well-being and needs isn't selfish. To actually support other people, we have to be in good health ourselves and have a strong sense of well-being. Keep this in mind when you are ploughing so much into the needs of others.

ENVIRONMENT

We spend so much time in our workplaces that we need to ensure that the environment is fit for purpose for both adults and children. Some of the essential elements will be the same for our children and our adults. It is important that we all work in a clean and tidy working atmosphere; this should be one of the most basic requirements. Simple things like making sure that there is soap in toilets and paper towels in the dispensers, and that the bins are emptied are vital. When these essential elements slip, standards slip, so ensure that your premises officer knows the expectations and the impact of this. High expectations of a clean and healthy environment, including an exciting learning environment, will need to be backed up by ensuring that children have the correct equipment provided by school and adults have the resources that they need to complete their job to a high, effective standard. Remove petty arguments from within your environment over late payments for tea and coffee facilities, and simply make the items free. If we cannot provide refreshments for our staff free of charge, then that's a real worry, especially with how quick and acrimonious an argument can become over the cost of semi-skimmed milk. It really isn't worth the bother.

WORKING WITH COLLEAGUES

The beauty of having so many colleagues is that everyone is different. The difficulties of having so many colleagues is that everyone is different. Personalities clash, which is inevitable, but at all points of the day we have to remember that we have the biggest thing in common with even our most opposite colleague: we care about their outcomes and the progress of our children. To promote well-being with colleagues, two initiatives are widespread on Twitter that have a high impact on injecting positivity into the workplace:

- Shonette Bason Wood shared a concept called 'Spread the Happiness'. It involves injecting happiness into the lives of our colleagues through any ways you can: giving them £1 that they need for parking, making them a coffee or offering to do a break duty. They then will be able to 'spread the happiness' further to other colleagues. This initiative can be adapted to children and they can do something nice for another child who can then pass this forward. This can be something simple like writing a nice note, commenting on someone's personality or character – e.g., 'Ben, you are a fantastic friend and I like the way you always ask me to play with you at breaktime' or 'Joe, thanks for being understanding when I am late to band practice. I will try and do better in the future.'
- The other initiative is by Abbie Mann and involves well-being bags. A colleague could make a well-being bag for another colleague. They can be as low cost or as luxurious as

you like. You may even be able to make them free by contacting local businesses. They can contain things that will cheer up or support your colleagues.

EXAMPLES OF WHAT COULD GO INSIDE A WELL-BEING BAG

- My book that you're reading now :-)
- A mug – tea solves every problem always.
- Teabags – because you must never be caught short.
- Penny – because they are lucky and you can always use a bit of luck within a school setting.
- Chocolate – because sometimes you just need it.
- Fragrant candle and/or a soothing bath soak.
- Stationery – because teachers love stationery – and who can frown at free post-it notes?
- A handwritten card – it has to be handwritten, as it shows that you have put time and thought into the words contained within it.

You could also complete these for your children at particularly stressful times, such as exam periods. Adjust the contents to suit the requirements of the age of your children. A well-being bag for a child about to embark on their GCSEs will be different from a well-being bag for a child about to embark on the Year 6 SATS.

STRATEGIES AND IDEAS FOR MANAGING YOUR WORKLOAD

Aside from behaviour, workload is another major reason cited for teachers leaving the profession, so it is important to be mindful. We can't change the job. It is what it is, but it is important to have certain systems in place to ensure that you are being as time efficient as you can and are balancing your workload effectively. Consider the following:

- One-to-one well-being meetings – we mentioned these previously, so I won't describe them in detail again, but they will enable you to really understand the specific issues within your workplace so you can strategise to support them.
- PPA (planning, preparation and assessment) time – needs to be in year groups, phases or subjects. This will maximise effectiveness. You can share the workload, which would be the biggest advantage, but do not underestimate the power of having someone to bounce ideas off.
- Emails – seriously consider not putting work emails on your phone. I appreciate it seems like a good idea at the time, but if you check your work emails on your phone, it means you are accessible at all times of the day, including during family time, and this is where it can have the most impact on your well-being. While we're on the subject of emails, set a time limit. We all have different lives and commitments, and we may need to answer emails at different times. To ensure that you're not having a negative impact on others, arrange for your staff to set times on their email accounts where they are happy to receive emails – e.g., between 8.00 am and 5.00 pm on weekdays.

Must follow on Twitter:

@thosethatcan – Dr Emma Kell is a secondary teacher who has completed much research on well-being.

Thank You – Template

Write a colleague a thank you card and share it with them.

e**X**CLUSION

Mention the word 'exclusion' on Twitter and you will receive a huge number of replies from streams of people, who are either very pro-exclusion or very anti-exclusion. It can be very hard to wade through these replies to actually find out about exclusion. It can also be very intimidating to try to ask simple questions when you are in this situation, without worrying about being pounced on. In this entry, we will explore exclusion, the different forms of exclusion, and your involvement, and I will try to answer any questions that you may have. It is important to note that exclusion is the *last resort*, so you may have this book for a few years before you even need to come back and re-read this entry. All the other entries are there to support you so that you do not even get to this point. There are four areas that we will discuss first, but it is important to note that when you are working with exclusions, you must check the up-to-date guidance provided by the Department for Education.

The four areas we will look at first are:

- fixed-term exclusions;
- permanent exclusions;
- managed moves;
- alternative provision.

Whenever we discuss exclusion, one of the main questions that I hear asked is, 'What gets a child excluded?' There is never a simple or consistent answer to this. The response that I would say is that you would need to look at the behaviour policy of the school to be able to answer it correctly. All schools must have their behaviour policy online. Details of the exclusion process, including examples of behaviours that could cause this process being activated, should also be detailed there, so this would give you an example of an answer to that common question. Fixed-term exclusions and permanent exclusions rarely come out of the blue for a one-off incident. Schools have usually worked with a family and a child through the processes that we have discussed, and will have involved different agencies, spent time acting on their advice, and completed interventions on an assess, plan, do and review cycle, and so on.

FIXED-TERM EXCLUSIONS

An extremely important point to note is that only the head teacher has the legal power to exclude. Fixed-term exclusions are a sanction imposed for a behaviour (which must be detailed in a school's behaviour policy *and* published online). It is a short period of time when a child is unable to come to school as a consequence of their behaviour. It can be for parts of the day – e.g., lunchtimes. However, it is important to note that a lunchtime exclusion is the same classification for a half-day exclusion. When the decision has been made to exclude on a fixed-term basis, it is the duty of the head teacher to inform all parties. Without delay, the parents must be informed, in writing, of the reason for the fixed-term exclusion, the period of fixed-term exclusion, the parents' right to appeal the decision, how this appeal needs to be made, that children cannot be seen in public during school hours, and how representations can be made at appeals. This letter needs to be given to the parents or posted to their last known address. If the period of exclusion is for over five days, then the school needs to provide alternative education from the sixth day, which also needs to be detailed.

A fixed-term exclusion cannot be converted into a permanent exclusion unless new evidence has come to light after the fixed-term exclusion was imposed. The legal limit of accumulated time for fixed-term exclusions is 45 days. On approaching this limit, it is important that the head teacher considers all options before thinking about the possibility of a permanent exclusion.

PERMANENT EXCLUSION

This is self-explanatory. If a child receives a permanent exclusion, they are no longer to be educated in the setting that they have been excluded from. Informing parents would run alongside the same guidelines as a fixed-term exclusion. Ensure that you read the exclusion guidelines before you consider either a fixed-term or permanent exclusion to have the most up to-date guidance.

MANAGED MOVES

A managed move can often be an alternative to a permanent exclusion. It is a voluntary agreement between two schools and the parents of the child that will allow a child to move schools under a controlled agreement. With a managed move, no exclusion will be recorded on a child's record. The advantages of a managed move are for a child to have a fresh start in a new setting, all parties are involved with the choice and can control how it is done and processed, and transition can mean that there is as little disruption to the child's education as possible. If you are considering a managed move for a child in your school, speak to the exclusions teams at your county council, who will be able to provide up-to-date support on the legalities around transition. As a basic, the transition during the managed move should include key information on when it should be, where it should be and the next steps, an adjusted individual education plan for the child, the named people responsible for implementing the plan, and incentives and goals for achievements under the agreement.

CASE STUDY - Primary

Joe was at risk of exclusion from his primary school for persistent disruptive behaviours. He had been at his primary school for four years. Relationships had broken down between the school and his family and he was continuing to exhibit behaviours that were causing complaints from other parents. The senior leadership team felt that they had no further option but to exclude him. Alternative provision discussed a managed move as an option. Joe felt that his primary school didn't trust him or believe that he could behave, so he didn't feel that he should try. A fresh start in another mainstream school could be an option, so it was decided to link with another local school. Alternative provision worked with Joe, the current primary school and the primary school that he was transitioning to in order to look at an effective transition plan. Joe moved to his new school with a fresh start and was able to reintegrate in to mainstream school effectively, without permanent exclusion.

ALTERNATIVE PROVISION

The thought of alternative provision certainly shouldn't be a final resort, and there is a lot of expertise to enhance mainstream provision for the outcomes of our children. The majority of behaviour alternative provisions, such as Pupil Referral Units, offer outreach services, behaviour panels, etc., so you can work with them from the very beginning.

I hope now that we are at the end of this entry, your questions and queries on exclusion have been answered. Something which you need to be aware of (if you aren't already) is that informal exclusions – sending children home to cool off, etc. – are illegal and should not happen in our schools.

Must follow on Twitter:

@jarlathobrien – a useful resource for information on exclusions and research.

Managed Move

This will need to be completed by the home school and be brought to the Initial Managed Move meeting

Child's name:		School:		

	Overall Good	Overall Satisfactory	Overall Poor
Attainment			
Effort			
Attitude to staff			
Attitude to peers			
Homework			

Reasons for Managed Move: Why might a move to this particular school be successful?

SEN	LAC status	Ethnicity	Attendance	Exclusions

Outside Agency Involvement	Impact/Additional Information

Additional Information

Yellow
(MENTAL HEALTH)

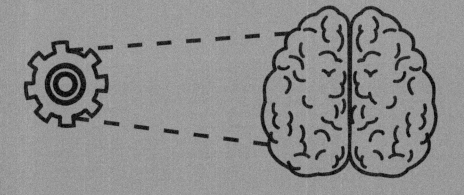

A lot of work has been completed recently which has looked at mental health in schools and how we can best support our children. Yellow is the colour that signifies support with mental health awareness days, so I felt it was appropriate for this entry to be yellow.

The Mental Health and Well-being entries in this book go hand in hand with each other, as they should as themes in a school. The effective teaching of mental health and emotional well-being in a school's Personal, Social, Health and Economic (PSHE) education curriculum not only plays a vital role in keeping pupils safe throughout their lives, it also provides them with vital skills that will enable them to be successful in their lives. We must think about how we can support both our colleagues and our children, but ultimately, if we can help our children to develop healthy coping strategies, to be able to remain resilient in the face of adversity and to understand their own emotions as well as those of others, then we will have done our job successfully.

We have always taught to support the needs of mental health, but not explicitly. It has always featured in the PSHE curriculum, but now we are able to teach this in a specific way. When the guidance was first released that we were to teach that mental health should be supported, there was an outcry of worry. Teachers felt daunted – and I completely understand that – but with statistics indicating that one in five children will be affected by mental health issues, we must do something to support our children (see www.mentalhealth.org.uk/a-to-z/c/children-and-young-people). There are, however, some incredibly challenging and sensitive areas of mental health and emotional well-being, so, if sufficient background knowledge is low in these areas, please seek training before you embark on teaching. We certainly wouldn't want to damage anyone further by naively embarking on teaching a subject or an area where we are lacking the required knowledge and skills.

The majority of learning related to mental health and emotional well-being is often taught to older children, particularly upwards of Key Stage 4 (ages 14–16), but there has been a shift to teaching this to children at a much younger age. Just as with musical tuition, vocabulary, languages, etc., building up from the early years is most effective. Even if a school can only look at this on enrichment days, it is much better than a child not having any awareness of mental health.

DATES FOR WHOLE-SCHOOL EVENTS

January – Young Carers Awareness Day (usually towards the end of the month)

May – Mental Health Awareness Week (usually the week commencing the second Monday in May)

October – Mental Health Awareness Month

These events are a great way of bringing awareness on a whole-school level. The dates will change year on year, so please make sure that you check their websites to have these before you plan your events calendar.

The promotion of positive behaviours and strategies early on in a child's school life can help them when they face physical or emotional adversity. The links in PSHE lend themselves perfectly to teaching about mental health and emotional well-being, with topics such as making friends and developing relationships, keeping safe, and experiences at home, in the community and in the wider world. There are a series of protective facts, which can reduce the risk of pupils moving from healthy coping mechanisms to unhealthy coping mechanisms, such as self-harm, substance misuse and eating disorders. These include:

- good communication skills;
- good problem-solving skills;

- healthy coping skills (including healthy responses to moments of crisis);
- the knowledge, skills and confidence to seek help;
- the ability to understand a range of emotions, and the ability to manage emotions, friendships and relationships well;
- understanding what positive self-esteem is;
- having an appreciation of difference and uniqueness;
- an experience of and an ability to manage failure.

So much of our curriculum lends itself to supporting the development of the protective factors at an early age. Other areas can feel that they should be taught discretely, but learning opportunities may appear at different points in school.

We have discussed in previous entries the promotion of character education and the development of these key learning values or characteristics. This goes hand in hand with promoting a growth mindset in school. We need to support our children to feel in control of their learning, so that they can get better and reach their goals, and know that with effort and perseverance, they can learn anything. A word of warning, though: schools can have attractive growth mindset displays in school, but actually facilitating children to have 'growth mindset' attitudes in themselves is something that takes time, explicit teaching and encouragement.

Knowing what to teach and when is different in different contexts. Certain mental health difficulties can be more prevalent in different cohorts of children. Also, facts show (see www.mentalhealth.org.uk/sites/default/files/fundamental-facts-about-mental-health-2016.pdf) that children are most vulnerable from about the age of 12, and the peak in the beginnings of self-harm and eating disorders is at about the ages of 14–15. This doesn't lead us to plan education around these issues at this time, but indicates that we need to educate our children beforehand, so that they are prepared and informed before these issues become prevalent.

OTHER ELEMENTS IN YOUR SCHOOL THAT SUPPORT DEVELOPING PROTECTIVE FACTORS IN PSHE

- Ground rules of a lesson – these need to be consistently kept to, revisited and reinforced. An understanding of confidentiality in lessons needs to be discussed as well. You may want to have something similar to the following:
  - All ideas/thoughts/feelings are correct.
  - There are no wrong answers.
  - We respect everybody's thoughts, ideas and feelings.
  - When we share our thoughts/ideas/feelings in this room, we don't then share them with our friends.
- Open conversations – children need to understand that they can ask any questions about mental health or emotional well-being in your lesson. Be mindful of safeguarding and ensure that children's safety is paramount.
- Non-judgemental attitudes in lessons.
- The right not to participate in discussions – children need to know that they do not have to voice their opinions in a session if they feel uncomfortable and that they can simply engage by listening.

Mental health cannot be summarised in a short entry in this book, but I hope I've given you a starting point from which you can reflect on how you can help in the best possible way. There are a variety of agencies that can support you further:

- the Department of Education (see its Further Education guidance on mental health in classrooms, which can be found at https://assets.publishing.service.gov.uk/government/uploads/system/uploads/attachment_data/file/755135/Mental_health_and_behaviour_in_schools__.pdf);
- YoungMinds;
- Action for Children;
- Time to Change.

It could include strategies to improve the school's provision of Healthy Schools (which now includes mental health), as well as ideas for good PSHE practice and schemes of work such as Jigsaw.

Must follow on Twitter:

@YoungMindsUK – the UK's leading charity for mental health in young people

What's On Your Mind?

This activity is designed to open up communication with someone over the stresses they are currently feeling. It is a common symbol for the things that you hold in your mind, so encourage children to draw or write about their current stresses. Discuss those feelings/ideas individually or create a block of work around them, depending on how many there are.

The activity is designed to promote discussion, but also to take each of the stressors one at a time and then to come up with strategies together to tackle them in an appropriate manner.

Well, we're at the end – or are we? This book is designed to make it easy for you to keep coming back for short bursts of inspiration when you need them. One of the strongest support networks that you can have is your group of colleagues. Working in that supportive atmosphere is more powerful and more supportive than any other option in teaching. It can make a huge difference to well-being, workload and happiness within your job and workplace. Trust is key to this; it is incredibly hard to build, but quick to break and difficult to repair. To know how to build trust and ensure a supportive working atmosphere, you need to have no illusions about what the current school climate is. You need to hear and be open to everybody's opinions: those of other school staff, parents, children and the teachers in your school.

One way of feeling the buzz in your school is to ask parents to complete online surveys via one of the free platforms such as SurveyMonkey. Be wary of the negatives of using this approach – e.g., not being able to follow this up to find out more – and make sure that you allow everyone to access the online survey by providing opportunities for use of computing equipment, etc. Some schools have paper copies of surveys available for people to take away on parents' evening. This is a better way of ensuring that you get more replies and, therefore, a better indication of the actual opinions of your key stakeholders. You could even use the replies from your one-to-one well-being meetings to gauge the opinions of your staff.

Once you know what the honest opinions of all the stakeholders are, you can strengthen your positives and improve your weaknesses where you can. Sometimes, your weaknesses aren't something that you actually have the power to improve but, if so, then you can be honest and transparent about it. Look at the replies and choose three positives to share, and no more than five things that you can focus on improving. If you just focus on the areas in which you can improve, then you will run the risk of being negative in your quest for improvement. People will forget the positives. Don't let them.

Create your shared vision with all stakeholders. You know from working with your children that when rules and ideas come from everybody, they are much more effective. Allow pupil voice to be paramount. Support and encourage the children to be vocal in school improvement and in improving outcomes for their peers, as well as encouraging stakeholders to be honest in their vision for school improvement. When colleagues and children feel that they are being heard and see that you are being honest and transparent, a positive school environment will be created and your school will have that 'buzz' of community.

School staff need to (and I'm sure that they do) understand that pupil well-being and outcomes are at the heart of the school environment, but this can all be done with a sense of fun. By fun, I don't mean those team-building days – which look amazing, by the way – but small actions that will inject a smile on a regular basis into your school.

Here are some ideas:

- Write the name of each member of staff on a piece of paper. Share them around and encourage each member of staff to write a positive affirmation about that person on the pieces of paper. Once every piece of paper has gone round, each member of your school staff will have a piece of paper detailing how fantastic everybody thinks they are and it will have specific praise on there. This is also a fantastic activity to complete with your children during a PSHE (Personal, Social, Health and Economic) education session or during tutor time.

- Have a staff shout-out board. Erect a display board in a communal area where anybody on the school staff can pop a post-it note to thank someone for something that they have done that week. This has a wonderful effect on people's self-worth and self-esteem, as well as boosting your positive school climate. Again, this is a fantastic activity that you can do with the children. However, I would make a slight change. Instead of a public board, have a closed box where the children can post notes. This isn't because their praise should be hidden. Some children struggle with praise and, as their teacher, you can check beforehand which one you pull out and share, and which praise needs to be given on a one-to-one basis.

- CPD (continuing professional development) library – place a bookcase in a communal space and share your educational book once you have completed it. It not only means that you can retrieve it and refer to it at school, but you can share it with other colleagues who can get the benefits of it too. I think most classrooms have a sharing bookcase but, if not, this is an invaluable strategy to try out with your class. The children love to borrow something that you recommend and are more likely to use it, as well as feeling valued that you have lent them something.

- Encourage strong relationships amongst staff – e.g., chip-shop Friday is a great way of getting colleagues to eat together and subsequently develop strong relationships, or have a departmental night out or activity such as bowling.

Try to keep that 'buzz' going. If you take your eyes off it, then it becomes stale. It isn't the responsibility of one person to create a positive working environment; it is the responsibility of all who work there and it's certainly worth doing because once it's established, then everybody will benefit.

TOP FIVE TIPS FOR CREATING A 'BUZZY' SCHOOL

You're never going to have a great day every day. It's just not the way it works, but if you can create a school with a great atmosphere, then your colleagues will boost you when you need it and you can create a similar environment for them as well. Use the following tips to form a supportive environment that everyone wants to work in:

1. Be open – create a culture where everyone is welcome. If people want to come and see your everyday classroom, allow them in. Let people come and see the learning with the children. It might take time for people to trust that this isn't about accountability but, once established, you will have an environment that will be nothing but supportive.

2. Be genuine with your interactions – I could quite easily say 'Know everyone's name' and 'Say hi to everybody', which of course is nice, but if it isn't genuine, then there really isn't any point. Get to know everybody and they will do this in turn.

3. Offer help – when people are struggling, more often than not they won't ask for help. Know your colleagues, see when they are tired or struggling, and just muck in and help. I appreciate that this will add more to your workload, but, rest assured, they will be the first to turn around and help you when you need it.

4. Have fun! – work is work and things need doing, but if you can't have fun with your colleagues, then the days will become dreary and monotonous.

5. Ask for ideas – it is quite easy to get lost in your vision of what is right, what is wrong and what is best. You are not alone in the school, and it's important to listen to the ideas that others have. People feel valued when you listen to their ideas, and are on cloud nine when you actually take them on, so take the time to ask.

Must follow on Twitter:

@chrisdysonHT – Chris Dyson is an inspirational head teacher with a positive school environment and buzz within his school.

Solution-focused Problem Template

Problem

Initial solution	Barriers	Final solution to present

I know that when my colleagues read this section they will laugh, as I am of the mindset that if they are coming to me with a problem, I expect them to have an idea of a solution.

This solution-focused problem template will allow ownership for colleagues, but also support a team approach when working with the daily problems we face.

Use the top box to write the problem you have. We usually always have an initial solution, so the next box is for jotting that down.

Then think through the barriers that this initial solution may have, so you can have some thoughts around how they can be overcome or whether there is another solution that you may need to identify.

Then come up with your final solution.